CARDINAL NEWMAN

THE LIVING THOUGHTS LIBRARY

NEWMAN

THE LIVING THOUGHTS OF

CARDINAL NEWMAN

PRESENTED BY

HENRY TRISTRAM

OF THE ORATORY

THE LIVING THOUGHTS LIBRARY
Edited by Alfred O. Mendel

DAVID McKAY COMPANY, INC.
New York

THE LIVING THOUGHTS LIBRARY

Foreign rights have been acquired by publishers in the following countries: Argentina (Spanish), Brazil (Portuguese), Bulgaria, Denmark, Finland, France, Great Britain, Holland, Norway, Rumania, Sweden, Yugoslavia.

The portrait of Cardinal Newman is from a painting of 1889 by Emmeline Deane in the National Portrait Gallery, London.

Nihil obstat:
Henricus Franciscus David, B.A., D.D.
Censor Deputatus

Imprimatur:
✠Humphreius Bright
Vicarius Capitularis
Birmingamiae, die 11ª Junii, anno 1946

MANUFACTURED IN THE UNITED STATES OF AMERICA

TO
MY SISTER
AS A TOKEN OF
A DEBT UNPAID

John Henry Newman (1801–1890) was born in London, the eldest of six children. His father was a banker ; his mother came of a well-known Huguenot family.

John Henry Newman was educated at a private school at Ealing, and was entered at Trinity College, Oxford, in 1816 ; he graduated B.A. in 1820, and was elected Fellow of Oriel in 1822. Two years later he was ordained and, in 1828, became vicar of St. Mary's, Oxford. By this time Newman was one of the most prominent men in the religious and intellectual life of the university. In 1833 he began the *Tracts for the Times* and became one of the originators of the Oxford Movement. The publication of Tract 90 (1841) brought about a crisis in the Movement. In 1843 Newman resigned from St. Mary's, and thereafter it was only a matter of time until he made his submission to the Catholic Church (1845). He was ordained priest in 1847, while in Rome, and on his return home he established, by Papal Brief, the Oratory of St. Philip Neri in England on February 1, 1848. In 1849 part of the Community migrated to Birmingham, part to London ; he himself settled in Birmingham, and there spent the rest of his life.

In 1864 an ill-advised attack by Charles Kingsley gave Newman the opportunity of explaining his views in the *Apologia pro Vita Sua*, which finally established his position in the minds of his fellow-countrymen and, incidentally, took its place among the classics of English literature. In 1879 Newman was created Cardinal Deacon of St. George in Velabro.

Life travels upward in spirals. He who takes pains to search the shadows of the past below us, then, can better judge the tiny arc up which he climbs, more surely guess the dim curves of the future above him.

ABBREVIATIONS

Apo. .	.	*Apologia pro Vita Sua*
A.R. .	.	*Addresses to Cardinal Newman with his Replies*
D.A. .	.	*Discussions and Arguments*
Dev. .	.	*The Development of Christian Doctrine*
H.S. .	.	*Historical Sketches*
Idea. .	.	*The Idea of a University*
M. .	.	*Letters and Correspondence of John Henry Newman*, edited by Anne Mozley
O.S. .	.	*Sermons on Various Occasions*
P.S. .	.	*Parochial and Plain Sermons*
Prepos.	.	*The Present Position of Catholics*
S.E. .	.	*Stray Essays on Controversial Points*
U.S. .	.	*Oxford University Sermons*
V.M. .	.	*Via Media*
W. .	.	*The Life of John Henry Cardinal Newman*, by Wilfrid Ward

PREFACE

FOR THE BETTER PART OF A CENTURY NEWMAN HAS BEEN a chosen prey of the anthologist. During that period volumes, large or small, not always in English, of selections from his works have appeared, and that with increasing frequency. When the earliest of these projects was mooted, he raised no objection ; and it is hardly likely, however much he would have preferred his writings to be read as a whole, that he would have frowned upon its successors, perhaps least of all upon this, which happens to come from his own Oratory, and is thus in a sense the fulfilment of a design entertained in his own lifetime.

Those who have before me undertaken a similar task, have adopted their own individual lines of approach, and have made their selections accordingly. If the addition of this small volume to theirs needs any justification, it will be found in the principle that has determined the choice of extracts. Newman being so multifarious in his interests, it proved to be impossible to make within a small compass a selection of representative passages, and imperative to adopt a particular standpoint, and to adhere to it rigidly. That standpoint was fixed by a memory, not my own, from his extreme old age, which illustrates his vivid awareness of the fact that the trend of contemporary thought was steadily moving away from Christianity. One who was present on the occasion recorded his words, and reports them thus : " One evening he was talking quietly about the progress of unbelief. He anticipated a time when the world at large would assume that Christianity had been disproved. Those who persisted in believing in it would neither be listened to nor reasoned with. What would be said to them amounted to this : ' It has been disproved, we cannot disprove it again.' The tone of anger and impatience he put into his voice just for the moment it took to say these words, is the reason why a not otherwise remarkable conversation is remembered by one person who was present, nearly a quarter of a century afterwards." The deep feeling that suffused his remark on this occasion arose from his steadfast conviction from first to last that it was his supreme mission in life to stem, as far as it lay in his power, the tide of unbelief and to dissipate what seemed to him to be the " terrible deceit of these latter days." For this reason I have limited my attention to his protracted struggle against the " doctrine that there is no positive truth in religion," or " liberalism," as he called it, which from tentative beginnings in his earlier years continued to gather strength during the course of his life, and has become the great menace of to-day.

The alternative to " liberalism " is not obscurantism, although this is the common assumption. Granted the fact of Revelation, then in Newman's epigrammatic words, " Religion cannot but be dogmatic ; it ever has been." The theology of the Catholic Church is another alternative, and that, the growth of many centuries, is a highly organized and closely-knit intellectual construction. Remove dogma, and the whole edifice of religion falls to the ground ; or, as Newman put it in 1835, " the so-called religion of the heart, without orthodoxy of doctrine, is but the warmth of a corpse, real for a time, but sure to fail." This is more obvious now than it was when he uttered this warning more than a century ago ; and it is consoling to find, not only this particular statement confirmed, but Newman's general attitude justified by a thinker of such distinction as Professor Whitehead. " The witness of history," he has written, " and of common sense tells us that systematic formulations are potent engines of emphasis, of purification, and of stability. Christianity would long ago have sunk into a noxious superstition, apart from the Levantine and European intellectual movement, sustained from the very beginning until now. This movement is the effort of Reason to provide an accurate system of theology. . . . Thus the attack of the liberal clergy and laymen, during the eighteenth and nineteenth centuries, upon systematic theology was entirely misconceived. They were throwing away the chief safeguard against the wild emotions of superstition."

It is with some misgiving that I have deliberately, though

sorely against my will, ignored the caution implicit in Mr. G. M. Young's words, that " no one would be so rash as to abridge or paraphrase Newman." Could any one be more conscious than I am that he can hardly be abridged without loss or paraphrased without misrepresentation ?

The opportunity being given me, I should like to acknowledge here the ever-increasing debt under which I lie to my brethren, the Fathers of the Birmingham Oratory, under whose guidance I have learnt to revere the memory of Newman—a debt which they would perhaps not admit, yet one which certainly I can never repay.

HENRY TRISTRAM

PRESENTING

JOHN HENRY NEWMAN

"THEY WHO KNOW ONLY HIS WORKS, KNOW THE LEAST part of him." [1] Such was the opinion expressed after Newman's death by the compiler of the best-known anthology of extracts from his writings,[2] who had enjoyed the privilege of his personal friendship, and had remained in close touch with him during the last two decades of his life. It is the epitome in a single sentence of what others have said at greater length, and it is confirmed by domestic tradition ; but it is quoted here, because it gives us the standpoint from which we must approach Newman as an author. The complimentary implication apart, he would not have quarrelled with it himself, for his attitude towards his works was one of singular detachment. They had all been produced " from hand to mouth," and hence, as he cheerfully confessed, they were full of grammatical slips, full also of gross blunders in matters of fact ; and as for his style he had consistently sacrificed sound to sense, his one object being to express his meaning clearly and exactly. It always seemed to him that writing was " a sort of operation," [3] or " a mental childbearing," [4] since it involved such distress, and even pain. Compliments left him unmoved, and in one of his last letters he apologized for his indifference by pleading " cantankerousness." " It is," he explained, " as if I could not bear to be praised."

In reality he was a man of action forced by circumstances to become a man of letters ; and he did not hesitate to show his dislike for " the mere literary *ethos*." His one aim in life being to advance the kingdom of God on this earth, he availed himself of all the resources at his command to effect his object ; and writing was to him a means of fulfilling his vocation, though not the highest. But even so, he could not write

---

[1] W. S. Lilly, *Essays and Speeches*, p. 100.
[2] *Characteristics from the Writings of J. H. Newman.*
[3] *W.*, I, 296. [4] *Ibid.*, II, 204

without a definite "call"; the office he happened to hold imposed a duty upon him to take up his pen, or some "occasion" or other demanded his intervention; and then finding the appropriate stimulus in the necessity of the moment, he acquitted himself worthily of the opportunity.[1]

It was a "sore point" with him in his later years that he had not marked out for himself a special field of research, and never strayed outside its boundaries. He could not but allow the plausibility of the criticism levelled against him, that "to be various is to be superficial." Yet it may be said that, although he trespassed upon a large number of disparate subjects, he always struck an individual note; originality in thought or expression is a characteristic of all that he wrote. He seemed to live in the past; but he was far from being an obscurantist. He kept himself *au courant* with the advance of contemporary thought. Yet he would have subscribed to Pascal's expression of contempt for "geometry," as being, although the highest exercise of the human mind, at its best an end unworthy of a man.[2] Religion remained from first to last his predominant concern, not so much theoretically, as a subject for speculation, but practically, with all its implications, as a life to be lived. It was this preoccupation that stamped, as others have observed, the "note of unity" upon his life, and made of it, as Burne-Jones wrote, "a great poem."[3]

We must not be misled by the apparent variety of Newman's literary output into regarding it as the external reflection of a jumble of heterogeneous interests. It is apposite here to recall Bergson's dictum, that no philosopher worthy of the name has said, or in fact has sought to say, more than one thing, and has said that one thing because he has grasped just that one point.[4] In Newman's case the diversity lies on the surface; beneath there is an underlying unity. His essential message may be compressed into the principle, enunciated in 1838, but held by him from early years, that "Christianity," being a religion based upon Revelation, "cannot but be dogmatic."[5]

---

[1] *W.*, II, 44.   [2] Brunschvigg, *Pensées et Opuscules*, p. 229.
[3] *Memorials*, II, 211.
[4] *Revue de Metaphysique*, November 1911 : *L'Intuition philosophique*.
[5] *D.A.*, p. 134.

His many books are only variations on this single theme. " I have," he declared in 1864, " changed·in many things : in this I have not. From the age of fifteen, dogma has been the fundamental principle of my religion : I know no other religion ; I cannot enter into the idea of any other sort of religion ; religion, as a mere sentiment, is to me a dream and a mockery. . . . What I held in 1816, I held in 1833, and I hold in 1864. Please God, I shall hold it to the end." [1]

In opposition to this conception of Christianity stood the " anti-dogmatic principle," [2] embodied in what he calls liberalism or latitudinarianism almost indifferently, but perhaps with slightly different shades of meaning, the intellectual attitude being emphasized in the former, the practical consequence in the latter. What he understood under the term " liberalism," will become clear in the sequel ; but his definition of latitudinarianism may be given at once, because it was less prominent in his polemic, liberalism being the form of the error with which owing to circumstances he was mainly brought into contact : " The Latitudinarian doctrine is this : that every man's view of Revealed Religion is acceptable to God, if he acts up to it ; that no one view is in itself better than another, or at least that we cannot tell which is the better. All that we have to do then is to act consistently with what we hold, and to value others if they act consistently with what they hold ; that to be consistent constitutes sincerity ; that where there is this evident sincerity, it is no matter [what we profess to be]. . . . Now, I can conceive such a view of the subject to be maintainable, supposing God had given us no Revelation. . . . [But] Revelation implies a something revealed, and what is revealed is imperative on our faith, *because* it is revealed. Revelation implies imperativeness ; it limits in its very notion our liberty of thought, because it limits our liberty of error, for error is one kind of thought." [3]

The cradle of liberalism at Oxford was Newman's own college, Oriel. Elected to a Fellowship there in 1822, he had his mind opened to the intellectual tendencies of the age by his seniors in the Common Room, men like Hawkins and Whately, the intellectual heirs of Eveleigh and Copleston, the former of

[1] *Apo.*, p. 49.   [2] *Ibid.*, p. 48.   [3] *D.A.*, pp. 129–32.

whom had led the movement for the reform of Oxford studies, while the latter had raised Oriel to a foremost position among the colleges of the University. These four men together with Arnold, Hampden, Baden Powell, and Blanco White, formed a group, which came to be designated by the title or nickname of the "Noetics." T. Mozley has left a lively description of the "Old Oriel School," as he calls it, in his *Reminiscences.* "Its most prominent talkers, preachers, and writers," he says, "seemed to be always undermining, if not actually demolishing, received traditions and institutions ; and whether they were preaching from the University pulpit, or arguing in common room, or issuing pamphlets on passing occasions, even faithful and self-reliant men felt the ground shaking under them." [1] Pattison in his *Memoirs,* likewise, singles out their destructively critical approach to all subjects as their distinctive characteristic : "The Noetics knew nothing of the philosophical movement which was taking place on the continent ; they were imbued neither with Kant nor with Rousseau, yet this knot of Oriel men was distinctly the product of the French Revolution. They called everything in question ; they appealed to first principles, and disallowed authority as a judge in intellectual matters. There was a wholesome intellectual ferment constantly maintained in the Oriel common-room." [2] Hence it was that R. H. Froude called Oriel the *Scholae Philosophiae Speculativae* [3] ; and that a friend remarked to Newman that "the . . . Common Room stank of Logic." [4]

It was once said of Arnold that " he wakes every morning with the impression that everything is an open question." [5] But he was not in residence when Newman became a member of the Common Room. Whately, however, was ; and he made Newman one of the " anvils," on which he hammered out his ideas. He was no less extreme than Arnold, and certainly far more original and brilliant, and even more aggressive. " It would not be possible," writes T. Mozley, " to describe now the terror his presence was sure to infuse among all who wished things to remain much as they were

---

[1] *Reminiscences of Oriel, etc.,* I, 19.　　[2] *Memoirs,* p. 79.
[3] *Remains,* I, 169.　　[4] *Apo.,* p. 169.
[5] Whitridge, *Dr. Arnold of Rugby,* p. 163.

in their own lifetime. Instead of being comforted and built up in the good old fashion, they were told they were altogether wrong, and must first retrace all their steps and undo all they had been doing. What was worse, the efficacy of the cure which had become necessary consisted in the hearers thinking it out for themselves." [1] That was the treatment applied to Newman ; Whately taught him to think and to use his reason to such good purpose that he toyed with the idea of dedicating his first book to him for having, in teaching him to think, taught him to think for himself.[2] Whately, too, was irreverent towards the past, calling the Fathers " certain old divines," latitudinarian in his creed, speaking of orthodoxy as " one's own doxy," and heterodoxy as " another's doxy " ; and contemptuous of party differences, designating the High Church and Low Church parties respectively Sadducees and Pharisees.[3]

Newman did not emerge from his association with Whately entirely unaffected. External observers set him down as a Noetic ; Froude, for example, who wrote of him in 1828, " He is a fellow that I like more, the more I think of him ; only I would give a few odd pence if he were not a heretic." [4] He himself refers to " the shadow of that liberalism which had hung over [his] course " [5] ; and admits his tendency " to prefer intellectual excellence to moral," and his drift " in the direction of the Liberalism of the day." [6] But he does not seem to have gone very far ; at the most he criticised some propositions of the Athanasian Creed as being " unnecessarily scientific," evinced a " certain disdain for Antiquity," which showed itself in " flippant language against the Fathers," and from Middleton, " imbibed a portion of his spirit." [7] But at no time had he any sympathy with Whately's " special theological tenets." [8] Even when he was most under his influence, " I had," he claims, " no temptation to be less zealous for the great dogmas of the faith, and at various times I used to resist such trains of thought on his part as seemed to me (rightly or wrongly) to obscure them." [9] At the end of 1827 his drift was suddenly checked by two misfortunes—his own illness and the death of his

[1] *Reminiscences of Oriel, etc.*, I, 19.   [2] *M.*, I, 141.
[3] *Ibid.*, I, 110.   [4] *Remains*, I, 232–3.   [5] *Apo.*, p. 25.
[6] *Ibid.*, p. 14.   [7] *Ibid.*   [8] *Ibid.*, p. 13.   [9] *Ibid.*, p .49.

youngest sister, Mary.[1] His "early devotion towards the Fathers returned"; and he began to "read them chronologically."[2]

T. Mozley records how Newman used to refer to the Noetics as "men who lash the waters to frighten the fish when they have made no preparation to catch them."[3] Oxford suspected that a "conspiracy" had been hatched at Oriel; but it was not so. They were simply at the mercy of their argumentative dexterity, and could not refrain from exhibiting it indiscriminately without regard to the subject under discussion, without thought of consequences. This was the "moral malady," of which they were the victims—"pride of reason." "In their day they did little more than take credit to themselves for enlightened views, largeness of mind, liberality of sentiment, without drawing the line between what was just and what was inadmissible in speculation, and without seeing the tendency of their own principles."[4] Hence it came about that "they unconsciously encouraged and successfully introduced into Oxford a licence of opinion which went far beyond them."[5] and fostered among themselves the "rudiments of the Liberal party,"[6] which after their day fought for, and eventually gained, the ascendancy in Oxford.

Liberalism, in the third decade of last century, "was the badge of a theological school, of a dry and repulsive character, not very dangerous in itself, though dangerous as opening the door to evils which it did not itself either anticipate or comprehend"[7]; liberty of thought, in itself good, may, when freed from restraint, pave the way for false liberty. Now Newman equates Liberalism with false liberty of thought. For him it means "the exercise of thought upon matters, in which, from the constitution of the human mind, thought cannot be brought to any successful issue, and therefore is out of place. Among such matters are first principles of whatever kind; and of these the most sacred and momentous are especially to be reckoned the truths of Revelation. Liberalism, then, is the mistake of subjecting to human judgment those revealed doctrines which are

[1] *Apo.*, p. 14.
[2] *Ibid.*, p. 25.
[3] *Reminiscences of Oriel, etc.*, I, 20.
[4] *Apo.*, p. 289.
[5] *Ibid.*, pp. 288–9.　　[6] *Ibid.*, p. 287.
[7] *Ibid.*, p. 261.

in their nature beyond and independent of it, and of claiming to determine on intrinsic grounds the truth and value of propositions which rest for their reception simply on the external authority of the Divine Word." [1] As thus defined, Liberalism is the practical equivalent of what he elsewhere calls Rationalism.

In Rome in 1833, when he took leave of Dr. Wiseman at the English College, he replied to the courteous invitation to return in the future with the words, " We have a work to do in England." [2] In Sicily a few weeks later, he made to his servant, who also nursed him during his illness, a similar remark, " I am sure God has some work for me to do in England." [3] He returned home like a man charged with a mission divinely given. It is then significant, as a clue to his own interpretation of the scope of his life-work, that in his *Biglietto* speech in Rome in 1879, he summed it up in this declaration : " I rejoice to say, to one great mischief I have from the first opposed myself. For thirty, forty, fifty years I have resisted to the best of my powers the spirit of Liberalism in religion." [4] His work was various, apparently heterogeneous ; but it was dominated by a single purpose, and had a single aim—to maintain the Christian Faith in its integrity, and in its integrity to hand it down to future generations.

He had glimpsed the danger to which Christianity was exposed as early as 1826, and in that year had drawn attention to it in his first University Sermon : " Although, then, Christianity seems to have been the first to give to the world the pattern of the true spirit of philosophical investigation, yet, as the principles of science are, in process of time, more fully developed, and become more independent of the religious system, there is much danger lest the philosophical school should be found to separate from the Christian Church, and at length disown the parent to whom it has been so greatly indebted. And this evil has in a measure befallen us." [5] Quoting this in a paper written in 1885, he added in explanation : " From the time that I began to occupy my mind with theological subjects I have been troubled at the prospect, which I considered to lie before us, of an intellectual movement against religion, so

[1] *Apo.*, p. 288. [2] *Ibid.*, p. 34. [2] *M.*, I, 428.
[4] *W.*, II, 460. [5] *U.S.*, p. 14.

special as to have a claim upon the attention of all educated Christians. . . . This grave apprehension led me to consider the evidences, as they are called, of Religion generally, and the intellectual theory on which they are based. This I attempted with the purpose, as far as lay in my power, not certainly of starting doubts about religion, but of testing and perfecting the proofs in its behalf. In literal warfare, weapons are tested before they are brought into use, and the men are not called traitors who test them. I am far indeed from being satisfied with my own performances ; in my *Apologia* I call them tentative." [1]

Dean Church describes the *Apologia* as the " history of a great battle against Liberalism " ; and under this term, as he proceeds to explain, he includes " the tendencies of modern thought to destroy the basis of revealed religion, and ultimately of all that can be called religion at all." [2] Thus he envisages the Tractarian Movement, although it took its rise in a political crisis, from Newman's individual standpoint ; but it may be doubted whether all, or even the majority, of the participants recognized the goal at which he aimed. The " fundamental principle of the Movement of 1833," as he saw it, was the " principle of dogma " [3] ; and the " vital question " for him was, " how were we to keep the Church from being liberalized ? " [4] The danger was acute ; for he felt that " if Liberalism once got a footing within her, it was sure of victory in the event " ; and that " Reformation principles were powerless to rescue her." [5] Minor differences lost their significance in face of the common peril : at the outset he ignored divergencies between rival schools of thought, and in his desire " to have a strong pull in union with all who were opposed to the principles of liberalism, whoever they might be," [6] he made his appeal to all men of good will without distinction. This fact clearly reveals his attitude towards the Movement : he had no thought of forming a party, and he repudiated the term, when applied to the Tractarians. Still less did he aspire to leadership. He was well aware that he did not possess the gifts for such a role ; he even admitted the justice of the taunt of a friend, who

[1] *S.E.*, p. 104. [2] *Occasional Papers*, II, 386. [3] *Apo.*, pp. 48–9.
[4] *Ibid.*, p. 30. [5] *Ibid.*, p. 31. [6] *Ibid.*, p. 42.

quoted against him his own words about St. Gregory Nazianzen :
" Thou couldst a people raise, but couldst not rule." [1] " This
is the true office of a writer," he once declared in the University
pulpit, " to excite and direct trains of thought." [2] That was
the function he allocated to himself, and in that he showed
himself to be Whately's genuine disciple. He encouraged men
to think, and, if they responded, to think correctly, about the
most momentous questions that can engage a man's attention
in this world.

To us who survey the Movement at this remove of time it
would seem as if the cause championed by Newman was from
the outset, although he did not anticipate failure until he was
close upon his retirement from Oxford, doomed to defeat. It
is clear that several converging causes, apart from the traditional
fear of Rome, contributed to this result. Chief among them
was the fact that the Tractarians, as a body, in spite of Newman's
unparalleled personal ascendancy over the older undergraduates
and the younger graduates, carried little or no weight in the
University, and utterly failed to enlist the sympathy of those
who directed its policy. Their attitude Dean Church describes
as one of " contemptuous indifference, passing into helpless and
passionate hostility." [3] The authorities, *i.e.*, the Heads of
Houses, with Dr. Routh of Magdalen as an honourable exception, " attacked and condemned the Tractarian teaching at
once violently and ignorantly," without any regard for the
main tradition of English theology, which was to most an
" unexplored and misty region," to some moulded by Whately's
discipline a legacy of thought worthy only of cold disdain.[4]
Blind to the issues involved in the controversy that had split
Oxford into two camps, they made it their object to crush the
Tractarians at all costs, and thus willy-nilly they played into
the hands of the Liberals, who formed the hard core of resistance
to Tractarianism. The rise to power of the Liberals is a startling
phenomenon. In the first quarter of the century the Noetics
dominated Oriel, but hardly affected the rest of the colleges ;
during the second the Liberals, who inherited their principles
and pushed to greater lengths the same line of corrosive thought,

[1] *Apo.*, p. 59.   [2] *U.S.*, p. 275.
[3] *Oxford Movement*, p. 243.   [4] *Ibid.*, p. 304.

grew into a powerful party with adherents in all the colleges, and at last came to dominate the University. " They represented a new idea," writes Newman, " which was but gradually learning to recognize itself, to ascertain its characteristics and external relations, and to exert an influence upon the University. The party grew, all the time that I was in Oxford, even in numbers, certainly in breadth and definiteness of doctrine, and in power. And, what was a far higher consideration, by the accession of Dr. Arnold's pupils, it was invested with an elevation of character which claimed the respect even of its opponents. On the other hand, in proportion as it became more earnest and less self-applauding, it became more free-spoken ; and members of it might be found who, from the mere circumstance of remaining firm to their original professions, would in the judgment of the world, as to their public acts, seem to have left it for the Conservative camp. Thus, neither in its component parts nor in its policy, was it the same in 1832, 1836, and 1841, as it was in 1845." [1]

Dean Church has remarked how the " theories and paradoxes " of the Noetics, although looked at askance in their day as " startling and venturesome, " would have seemed " cautious and old-fashioned " in comparison with the enunciations of their Liberal successors.[2] Their views, although he does not refer to them by name, Newman has summed up in the following passage written in 1845 : " That truth and falsehood in religion are but matter of opinion ; that one doctrine is as good as another ; that the Governor of the world does not intend that we should gain the truth ; that there is no truth ; that we are not more acceptable to God by believing this than by believing that ; that no one is answerable for his opinions ; that they are a matter of necessity or accident ; that it is enough if we sincerely hold what we profess ; that our merit lies in seeking, not in possessing ; that it is a duty to follow what seems to us true, without a fear lest it should not be true ; that it may be a gain to succeed, and can do no harm to fail ; that we may take up and lay down opinions at pleasure ; that belief belongs to the mere intellect, not to the heart also ; that we may safely trust to ourselves in matters of Faith, and

[1] *Apo.*, pp. 291–2. [2] *Oxford Movement*, pp. 17–8.

need no other guide—this is the principle of philosophies and heresies, which is very weakness." [1]

When he began to see with growing clarity of vision the goal towards which he was inevitably tending, then, as he confesses, his " most oppressive thought . . . was the clear anticipation, verified by the event, that it would issue in the triumph of Liberalism." [2] This is what actually came about. Routed by the forces of Liberalism, he withdrew from the unequal contest ; but, he is generous enough to admit, " I found no fault with the Liberals ; they had beaten me in a fair field." [3] " The Oxford Movement was broken," wrote M. Arnold, " it failed ; our wrecks are scattered on every shore." [4] Some, certainly the majority, remained loyal to the Anglicanism to which the Movement had introduced them ; some, relatively few, and they neither the most prominent nor the most weighty, followed Newman into the Catholic Church ; and some, again, drifted into Liberalism, notably M. Arnold, M. Pattison, and J. A. Froude, although they never ceased to venerate Newman. The catastrophe, according to Pattison, marked " an epoch in the history of the University " [5] ; the Liberals, flushed with their triumph, " were carried beyond all bounds, sought to change everything, questioned everything, and were impatient to throw the whole cargo of tradition overboard." [6]

During the agitation about the Reform Bill, Newman, fresh from the study of the Fathers, contrasted the Primitive Church and the " Establishment" of his own day. " Look on this picture," he said to himself, " and on that." [7] Did a similar contrast present itself to his mind between that same Primitive Church and the Catholic Church in the nineteenth century, when he came to know it, no longer from report as an extern, but from experience as one of the faithful ? The Church had not then surmounted the flood of infidelity let loose over Europe by the French Revolution ; it was passing through a time of " peculiar difficulty and delicacy," [8] as he wrote in 1854, and the worst was not yet. In country after country the Episcopate had lost in prestige and position. " But now

[1] *Dev.*, pp. 357–8.   [2] *Apo.*, p. 203.   [3] *Ibid.*, p. 214.
[4] *Culture and Anarchy* (Popular Edition, 1905), p. 23.   [5] *Memoirs*, p. 236.
[6] *Ibid.*, p. 239.   [7] *Apo.*, p. 31.   [8] *H.S.*, III, 143.

at length," he declared in a sermon in 1866, " by the operation of the same causes which have destroyed the power of the Bishops, the Holy Father too is in danger of losing his temporal possessions," [1]—and what was of infinitely greater consequence, his spiritual independence. It was a time, of which he might have said, as he said of the Reformation epoch, " when our Lord seemed to be asleep in Peter's boat." [2] The Church, as centred in Rome, as united under its visible head, the Pope, appeared to be in dire peril ; but as though to redress the balance, Catholicism was showing notable signs of vitality by its rapid development in countries on the periphery of its influence. The episode of the Temporal Power reached its climax in 1870, when Rome became the capital of a United Italy ; for half a century and more the Pope was a prisoner in the Vatican ; but the Vatican Council, in the persons of its assembled Bishops, drawn from every quarter of the globe, had borne witness to the universality of the Church, and given promise of a future more glorious than the immediate past.

The Liberalism arrayed against the Church on the Continent, although based upon the same fundamental principles, flaunted a programme at once more comprehensive and incomparably more extreme than the system which passed under the same name in England ; and the latter itself had a connotation far wider than what Newman understood by the term in his Oxford days. Openly professing to exalt the natural order to the belittlement or the total exclusion of the supernatural, continental Liberalism was in its manifestations, and they were uncompromising and violent, anti-clerical, anti-religious, purely secular. In this aspect it was in Papal documents denominated *Latitudinarismus* or *Indifferentismus* ; and year after year during his pontificate Pius IX fulminated against this with its allied evils in a long series of Allocutions, Encyclicals, Briefs, culminating in the famous Encyclical *Quanta Cura*, of December 8, 1864, with the still more famous *Syllabus* attached. In this the Papacy was popularly supposed to have turned its back upon the world of the day by its condemnation, as an error, of the principle that " the Roman Pontiff ought to come to terms with modern civilization." But the Church is never obscurantist

[1] *O.S.*, p. 293.   [2] *Ibid.*, p. 202.

in its teaching, as its critics imagine ; the term, " modern civilization " is intended in the sense in which it was used in the Allocution, *Jamdudum cernimus,* of March 18, 1861, as applicable to a " system invented to weaken and perhaps even destroy the Church " ; and that the Pope could not do other than condemn.

Newman was of the opinion that what was happening before his eyes, was no more than the prelude to an even more unhappy and desperate state of affairs. " As a fact, I know," reported A. de Vere in 1850, " that Newman . . . anticipates an unprecedented outburst of infidelity all over the world ; that to withstand it he deems his special vocation, and that he is quite annoyed at having to spend any time on Anglicanism." [1] In the situation, as it then presented itself to his mind, it seemed to him that the Church had a signal advantage, which it did not have in the Middle Ages, in the fact that its foes did not conceal their hostility. " Contrasting the two periods together," he wrote in 1854, " we may even say, that in this very point they differ, that, in the medieval, since Catholicism was then the sole religion recognized in Christendom, unbelief necessarily made its advances under the language and the guise of faith ; whereas in the present, when universal toleration prevails, and it is open to assail revealed truth, . . . unbelief in consequence throws off the mask, and takes up a position over against us in citadels of its own, and confronts us in the broad light and with a direct assault. And I have no hesitation in saying . . . that I prefer to live in an age when the fight is in the day, not in the twilight ; and think it a gain to be speared by a foe, rather than to be stabbed by a friend. . . . It is one great advantage of an age in which unbelief speaks out, that Faith can speak out too ; that, if falsehood assails Truth, Truth can assail falsehood." [2]

But the spirit shown by the authorities (although it must be remembered, in justice to them, that they were at the post of danger, whereas he was only an observer without responsibilities at a distance) did not equal his own ; and as the protracted struggle went on, his dissatisfaction grew with their passive acceptance of what may be called a state of siege. His pent-up feelings at last found expression in a remarkable passage

[1] *Memoir,* p. 182. [2] *Idea,* pp. 381–2.

in a letter of 1866 : " At present things are in appearance as
effete, though in a different way, (thank God), as they were
in the tenth century.   We are sinking into a sort of Novatianism. . . . Instead of aiming at being a world-wide power, we
are shrinking into ourselves, narrowing the lines of communion,
trembling at freedom of thought, and using the language of
dismay and despair at the prospect before us, instead of, with
the high spirit of the warrior, going out conquering and to
conquer.   Can anything be more unworthy of Christian
prelates than the laments . . . that no hope is left, that there
is no earthly power to aid the Holy See, and that it is all along
of that wicked Louis Napoleon ? . . . But the power of God
is abroad upon the earth, and He will settle things in spite of
what cliques and parties may decide.   I am glad you like my
sermon [1]—the one thing I wished to oppose is the coward
despairing spirit of the day." [2]

From Newman's own personal angle of interest the most
deplorable weakness of the Church—the decay of theological
learning—resulted from the secularization of the universities
and the disappearance of their theological faculties, which
followed upon the French Revolution.   In his *Dublin Discourses*
he spoke of a university " as being the special seat of that large
Philosophy, which embraces and locates truth of every kind
and every method of attaining it " [3] ; and hence he held that
a university has a unique and essential function to fulfil in the
life of the body politic.   Solitary individuals may contribute to
the advance of knowledge ; but it is better, even for the sake
of knowledge, that they should not be solitary, since " truth is
wrought out by many minds working together freely." [4]
Mutual support and mutual supervision safeguard the individual
not only against his own idiosyncrasies, but also against mis-
understandings on the part of authority.   " Perhaps a local
teacher, or a doctor in some local school, hazards a proposition,
and a controversy ensues.   It smoulders or burns in one place,
no one interposing ; Rome simply lets it alone.   Then it comes
before a Bishop ; or some priest, or some professor in some

[1] " The Pope and the Revolution," *O.S.*, pp. 281–316.
[2] *W.*, II, 127–8 (in part).
[3] Omitted from *Idea*.   [4] *W.*, II, 49.

other seat of learning, takes it up ; and then there is a second stage of it. Then it comes before a University, and it may be condemned by the theological faculty. So the controversy proceeds year after year, and Rome is still silent. An appeal perhaps is next made to a seat of authority inferior to Rome ; and then at last after a long while it comes before the supreme power. Meanwhile, the question has been ventilated and turned over and over again, and viewed on every side of it, and authority is called upon to pronounce a decision which has already been arrived at by reason. . . . It is manifest how a mode of proceeding, such as this, tends not only to the liberty, but to the courage, of the individual theologian or controversialist. Many a man has ideas, which he hopes are true, and useful for his day, but he is not confident about them, and wishes to have them discussed." [1] But he asked in 1851, answering his own question in the same sentence, " At this moment, where are our schools of theology ? a scattered and persecuted Jesuit school—one at Louvain—some ghosts of a short-lived birth at Munich—hardly a theologian at Rome." [2]

" Nor is religion ever in greater danger," he thought, " than when, in consequence of national or international troubles, the schools of theology have been broken up and ceased to be," since " Theology is the fundamental and regulating principle of the whole Church system." [3] When these words were written (1877), the great theologian, J. B. Franzelin, had already done much to restore the credit of theology, and Leo XIII was soon to inaugurate the scholastic revival. Newman's strictures, then, apply to the theologians of an earlier age, and to them apply mainly because they had failed in the obligation, incumbent on them, to keep their science abreast of contemporary thought ; but it was rather their apologetic that lagged behind the times, not their theology in the strict sense ; and in consequence the laity faced with specious objections found themselves unprovided with the answers. At Propaganda (1846-7) Newman realized that a philosophical system adequate to the needs of the day was the great desideratum, the current philosophy of the schools being, as he was told, made up of " odds and ends " ; and he optimistically inferred from the

[1] *Apo.*, p. 267.   [2] *W.*, I, 251.   [3] *V.M.*, I, xlvii.

Encyclical, *Qui pluribus,* of November 9, 1846, that the Pope himself was not insensitive to that need.[1] But he was forced to confess that the Roman theologians and philosophers " living in a place whose boast is that it has never given birth to heresy," had come to imagine that " proofs ought to be convincing which in fact are not." [2] It was a perpetual embarrassment to him that they would not squarely face the difficulties fermenting in the educated mind. " And your cut and dried answers out of a dogmatic treatise," he protested, " are no weapons with which the Catholic Reason can hope to vanquish the infidels of the day." [3] But those whose duty it was to grapple with the various problems arising as the focus of intellectual interest shifted, so far from realizing that nothing remains stationary in this world of change, seemed to him to be blissfully content with the legacy of past ages : " Our theological philosophers are like the old nurses who wrap the unhappy infant in swaddling bands or boards—put a lot of blankets over him—and shut the windows that not a breath of fresh air may come to his skin as if he were not healthy enough to bear wind and water in due measure. They move in a groove, and will not tolerate anyone who does not move in the same. . . . I come to see, more than I did, what an *irritabile genus* Catholic philosophers are—they think they do the free Church of God service, by subjecting it to an etiquette as grievous as that which led to the King of Spain being burned to cinders." [4] If they would not, or could not, look actual conditions in the face, then those who are not theologians or philosophers *de métier,* should not be discouraged from occupying the neglected field of study, and raising their experimental crops. It is conceivable that a writer's " errors are those which are inseparable accidents of his system or of his mind, and are spontaneously evolved, not pertinaciously defended. Every human system, every human writer, is open to just criticism. Make him shut up his portfolio ; good ! and then perhaps you lose what, on the whole and in spite of incidental mistakes, would have been one of the ablest defences of Revealed Truth . . . ever given to the world." [5]

[1] *W.,* I, 149.   [2] *Ibid.,* I, 247.   [3] *Ibid.,* II, 49.
[4] *Ibid.,* II, 254-5.   [5] *Idea,* p. 477.

But to return to England, for it was with England that he was chiefly concerned—here the position had gone from bad to worse, since he had opened the campaign against incipient Liberalism at Oxford. "The Liberalism which gives a colour to society now,"—he is writing in 1864—"is very different from that character of thought which bore the name thirty or forty years ago. Now it is scarcely a party ; it is the educated lay world. . . . At present it is nothing else than that deep, plausible scepticism, of which I spoke above, as being the development of human reason, as practically exercised by the natural man. The Liberal religionists of this day are a very mixed body, and therefore I am not intending to speak against them. There may be, and doubtless is, in the hearts of some or many of them a real antipathy or anger against revealed truth, which it is distressing to think of. Again ; in many men of science or literature there may be an animosity arising from almost a personal feeling ; it being a matter of party, a point of honour, the excitement of a game, or a satisfaction to the soreness or annoyance occasioned by the acrimony or narrowness of apologists for religion, to prove that Christianity or that Scripture is untrustworthy. Many scientific and literary men, on the other hand, go on, I am confident, in a straight-forward impartial way, in their own province and on their own line of thought, without any disturbance from religious difficulties in themselves, or any wish at all to give pain to others by the result of their investigations. It would ill become me, as if I were afraid of truth of any kind, to blame those who pursue secular facts, by means of the reason which God has given them, to their logical conclusions ; or to be angry with science, because religion is bound in duty to take cognizance of its teaching." [1]

This, as Newman saw it, was the society in which Catholic laymen had to take their place and live their life—at the worst sceptical, at the best indifferent to all religious belief, certainly to Catholicism. How adequately were they equipped for the ordeal that awaited them ? This was the question that he anxiously put to himself. The Church in England had then only recently emerged from the catacombs ; for three centuries

[1] *Apo.*, pp. 261–2.

Catholics had been excluded from the national life, thrown back upon their own society, and starved of educational facilities. There were, of course, notable, even remarkable, exceptions ; but it would not be untrue to say that the rank and file in all classes fell short intellectually of the general run of their countrymen, although the gap between them was not as great as that implied in W. G. Ward's taunting estimate : " When a Protestant meets a Catholic in controversy, it is like a civilised man meeting a barbarian." [1] Newman, while admitting that " it too often happens that the religiously disposed are in the same degree intellectually deficient," [2] took a more sober view, contenting himself with the observation that " as to the laity there is a great deficiency in the higher education." [3] In what may, for want of a better term, be called his *Journal*, although it is merely a school exercise book of no great length, in which he made occasional entries, he enlarged upon this theme. Thus, on January 8, 1860, he wrote as follows : " I have seen great wants which had to be supplied among Catholics, especially as regards education—and of course those who laboured under those wants, did not know their state—and did not see or understand the want at all—or what was the supply of the want—and felt no thankfulness at all, and no consideration towards a person who was doing something towards that supply, but rather thought him restless, or crotchetty, or in some way or other what he should not be." [4] On January 21, 1863, he recurred to the same topic, when he wrote : " To me conversions were not the first thing but the edification [5] of Catholics. So much have I fixed upon the latter as my object, that up to this time the world persists in saying that I recommend Protestants not to become Catholics. And, when I have given as my true opinion, that I am afraid to make hasty converts of educated men, lest they should not have counted the cost, and should have difficulties after they have entered the Church, I do but imply the same thing, that the Church must be prepared for converts, as well as converts prepared for the Church. . . . And Catholics in England, from their very blindness, cannot see that they are blind. To aim then

---

[1] *W. G. Ward and the Oxford Movement*, p. 437.　　[2] *Idea*, p. 485.
[3] From the undated draft of a letter.　　[4] *W.*, I, 577.　　[5] i.e., building up.

at improving the condition, the status, of the Catholic body, by a careful survey of their argumentative basis, of their position relatively to the philosophy and the character of the day, by giving them juster views, by enlarging and refining their minds, in one word, by education, is (in their view) more than a superfluity or a hobby, it is an insult. It implies that they are deficient in material points. Now, from first to last, education, in this large sense of the word, has been my line." [1]

In all this Newman had in mind solely the education of the laity ; his original idea of establishing a school of theology in England having been received without warmth by the authorities, he ceased to concern himself with the training of the clergy. " As far as I am aware," he explained in 1860, " I have not written anywhere one word in discussion of the education proper for the clergy." [2] Hence his " general views . . . drawn out in various works " must be considered as having " reference to the education of the Catholic gentry." His ideal of the educated Catholic layman he sketched in a lecture delivered in Birmingham in 1851 : " What I desiderate in Catholics is the gift of bringing out what their religion is. . . . I want a laity, not arrogant, not rash in speech, not disputatious, but men who know their religion, who enter into it, who know just where they stand, who know what they hold, and what they do not, who know their creed so well that they can give an account of it, who know so much of history that they can defend it. I want an intelligent, well-instructed laity ; I am not denying you are such already ; but I mean to be severe, and, as some would say, exorbitant in my demands, I wish you to enlarge your knowledge, to .cultivate your reason, to get an insight into the relation of truth to truth, to learn to view things as they are, to understand how faith and reason stand to each other, what are the bases and principles of Catholicism. . . . I have no apprehension you will be the worse Catholics for familiarity with these subjects, provided you cherish a vivid sense of God above, and keep in mind that you have souls to be judged and to be saved. . . . Ignorance is the root of all littleness ; he who can realise the law of moral conflicts, and the incoherence of falsehood, and the issue of perplexities, and the end of all things, and the Presence of the Judge, becomes, from the very necessity of the case, philosophical, long-suffering, and magnanimous." [1]

But Newman was to learn in the school of hard experience during the following years that the authorities were not sufficiently alive to the imperious necessities of the times to enter into his views with any warmth. " On both sides the Channel," he wrote to a colleague in the Catholic University, " the deep difficulty is the jealousy and fear which is entertained in high quarters of the laity. . . . Nothing great or living can be done except when men are self-governed and independent ; this is quite consistent with a full maintenance of ecclesiastical supremacy." [2]   In Ireland, he gained at first-hand the impression that laymen were treated " as little boys " [3] ; and he came to fear that, if the Archbishop of Dublin had his way in the University, the Professors would be " simply scrubs." [4] After his return to England, in an interview with his own Bishop, Dr. Ullathorne, he expressed his dissent from the latter's statement that " Catholics never had a doubt ; it pained them to know that things could be considered doubtful which they had ever implicitly believed."   " Looking at the educated laity as a whole, and in prospect," he remarked in comment, " I could not say that I thought their state satisfactory. . . . The Bishops, etc., did not see the state of the laity, e.g. in Ireland, how unsettled, yet how docile." [5] Again, in 1861, writing on the subject of Galileo, he protested against what seemed to be the general official attitude towards the more educated among them : " There was a class, and ever is a class, whose claims to consideration are too little regarded now, and were passed over then—I mean the educated class. . . . Men who have sharpened their intellects by exercise and study, anticipate the conclusions of the many by some centuries . . . and it is as clear to me that their spiritual state ought to be consulted for, as it is difficult to say why in fact it so often is not.   They are to be tenderly regarded for their own sake ; they are to be respected and conciliated for the sake of their influence over other classes.   I cannot help feeling that, in high circles, the

[1] *Prepos.*, pp. 390-1.   [2] *W.*, I, 367.   [3] *Ibid.*, I, 315.
[4] *Ibid.*, I, 367.   [5] *Ibid.*, I, 497.

Church is sometimes looked upon as made up of the hierarchy and the poor, and that the educated portion, men and women, are viewed as a difficulty, an encumbrance, as the seat and source of heresy ; as almost aliens to the Catholic body, whom it would be a great gain, if possible, to annihilate." [1]

The intellectual difficulties raised by the progress of science among thoughtful men continued to haunt Newman's mind, since he felt deeply the need that something should be done for them, and deplored the inadequacy of the little that was being done. More than ever he was in close touch with men sensitive to the dangers that might result from stagnation in thought on the part of Catholics. Years before, in Rome, when he was writing a preface for the French translation of his *University Sermons,* he proposed to insert a sentence to the following effect : " I am not maintaining what I say is all true, but I wish to *assist in investigating* and bringing to light *great* principles necessary for the day—and the only way to bring these out is *freely* to investigate, with the inward habitual intention (which I trust I have) always to be submitting what I say to the judgment of the Church." [2] In Dublin he included among the objects of the University that of " providing philosophical defences of Catholicity and Revelation." [3] Now again, with his wider experience and more intimate knowledge of what Catholics were thinking, he could not turn a deaf ear to the appeals of those who were harassed by difficulties or torn by doubts ; and this project revived in his mind. " I wish," he wrote in 1861, " to do my part in destroying the feverishness and nervousness which is abroad, the vague apprehensions of some coming discoveries hostile to faith, that spontaneous unwelcome rising of questionings and perplexities in the secret heart, which cut at the root of devotion, and dry up the founts of love, homage, loyalty, admiration, joy, peace, and all the other best and noblest attributes of religion. It is perfectly true that obedience is acceptable to God, and may even be heroic, when performed amid darkness, dryness, and dejection ; but few people except Saints can long endure so heavy a trial ; and I shall think myself most highly favoured

---

[1] From an unpublished manuscript   [2] *W.,* I, 173.
[3] Rector's Report, 1854-5.

by the God of grace and truth if He shall enable me to suggest anything useful to any one soul who is under this special visitation. If I attain this object by lawful means, I shall not stand in need of any other consolation." [1]

Pressure was brought to bear upon him, not only by Catholics, but even by Protestants, to induce him to write upon the burning topics of the day; but, although their persuasions coincided with his own wish, he was deterred by counsels of prudence. Firstly, he found it impossible to determine to his own satisfaction the exact lie of the land or to decide what precisely were the objections to be " encountered and overthrown." " I am far from denying," he admitted, " that scientific knowledge is really growing, but it is by fits and starts; hypotheses rise and fall; it is difficult to anticipate which of them will keep their ground, and what the state of knowledge in relation to them will be from year to year." [2]

Secondly, he did not think it wise to run the risk of official disapproval, since a " cuff from the political ultra-devotional party," [3] then firmly established in England, would undermine his own position, and not help to further the cause of intellectual freedom. " *I* should wish," he wrote in his *Journal* on January 21, 1863, " to attempt to meet the great infidel, etc., questions of the day; but both Propaganda and the Episcopate, doing nothing themselves, look with extreme jealousy on any one who attempts it, and, giving him no credit for what he does well, come down with severity on any point in which he may have slipped." Before the end of that year the Brief, *Tuas libenter,* addressed to the Archbishop of Munich, confirmed him in his view that the authorities would prefer that an attitude of reserve should be adopted on all scientific subjects. " I thought it was commonly said," was his comment, " that Galileo's fault was that he meddled with *theology,* and that, if he had confined himself to *scientific conclusions* he would have been let alone; but surely the language of the Brief . . . is as if even men of science must keep *theological* conclusions before them in treating of *science.* . . . I certainly could not write a word upon the special controversies and difficulties of the day

---

[1] From the unpublished manuscript quoted above.
[2] *Apo.,* pp. 262–3.   [3] *W.,* II, 374.

with a view to defend religion from free-thinking physicists without allowing them freedom of logic in their own science ; so that, if I understand this Brief, it is simply a providential intimation to every religious man, that, at this moment, we are simply to be silent, while scientific investigation proceeds—and say not a word on questions of interpretation of Scripture, etc., etc., when perplexed persons ask us." [1] In this conclusion he acquiesced, as not unlikely to " prove to be the best way," things being as they were. " So far from finding a difficulty in obeying in this case," he explained in the *Apologia*, " I have cause to be thankful and to rejoice to have so clear a direction in a matter of difficulty." [2]

Thirdly, having been once delated to Rome, he had little confidence in the discernment of the theologians of the schools, who would not grasp that his was an entirely individual approach, or that his object was no more than to supplement them. " Hannibal's elephants," he thus explained his silence, " never could learn the goose-step." [3] He had not passed through the theological mill, and was unable or unwilling to undo the mental habits of half a lifetime. Father Ignatius Ryder, who lived under him for more than forty years, has with a certain humour exposed the cause of the mutual suspicion. " It cannot be denied," he wrote, " that for a considerable time a feeling prevailed in certain high quarters, both in Rome and in this country, that Fr. Newman was a dangerous man. What precisely this might mean, was probably anything but clear to those who entertained the sentiment. The truth was, it was exceedingly difficult for men trained in the formal logic of the schools to understand one whose propositions lent themselves awkwardly to the discipline of mode and figure. . . . Then what seemed to them antilogics, troubled them. Fr. Newman was reserved and outspoken, ultramontane and liberal, uncompromising and minimistic. He was a formidable engine of war on their side, but they were distinctly aware that they did not thoroughly understand the machinery. And so they came to think, some of them, that it might perhaps one day go off of itself, or in the wrong direction." [4]

[1] *W.*, I, 642. [2] p. 263.
[3] *W.*, I, 579. [4] *W.*, I, 18 (in part).

The men who dominated the Church in England during that period, in particular Manning, Ward, and Vaughan, were not theologians in the strict sense. Ward, beyond all comparison the most competent of them, stood in the view of the Roman theologians as a typical autodidact ; and certainly in his tendency to run into extremes he betrayed the weakness of the self-taught man. Now Newman was not, any more than Ward, a theologian in the strict sense, although he could claim a year in Rome, as Ward could not [1] ; but before he put pen to paper, he had his authorities arrayed before him, and on no subject did he ever speak without book. " I don't profess to be a theologian," he granted, " but at all events I should have been able to show a side of the Catholic religion more theological, more exact, than his." [2] It was his jealousy for dogma in its integrity, that fired his antagonism to the "violent ultra party, which exalts opinions into dogmas, and has it principally at heart to destroy every school of thought but its own." [3] This noisy group of extremists with their " arrogant *ipse dixits*," who, like the " three Tailors of Tooley Street " [4] in another sphere, claimed to be the Church—Novatianism was the term he applied to their attitude [5]—made their voices heard, and their words were echoed in Rome through the mouth of Mgr. Talbot, a prominent ecclesiastic whose abilities were hardly on a level with his influence, which he exerted always to Newman's disadvantage. But it may well be that his diatribes carried less weight than they seem to have done ; and in any case his inanities scarcely deserve even a passing recognition here.

But Newman, as was almost inevitable, when he was being pilloried for " unsoundness and disloyalty," had to pay the penalty, not only for the exaggerated language of the more indiscreet among his friends, but, what was far worse, for the distortions of his opinions put out by minimisers who wished to shelter under his name. Fr. Ryder, who speaks here, as always, with authority, summed up the situation accurately, when he wrote : " The anxious consideration with which he treated every kind of religious difficulty, both inside as well as outside the Church ; his scrupulous abstinence from any conduct that might seem to partake of the character of premature excommunication, was sometimes taken advantage of by those whose interest it was to interpret his sympathy with their difficulties into a sympathy with their opinions. And there were not wanting busybodies on the other side, who exaggerated what they did not understand into something they were justified in disliking. All along there were very many in the highest places in the Church, whose sentiments towards him were those of unqualified admiration and confidence. And the rest, even those who were least in accord with him, to borrow a phrase from his philosophy, yielded a real assent to his merits, a notional assent to his short-comings." Perhaps it was his consciousness of this broad sympathy as more than a counterpoise to minor discords that prompted his gentle rebuke to a friend, whose opinions had been voiced too forcibly ; " You must hate, not theologians, but theologists."

There can be, of course, no doubt that, during all the years of his late maturity when his powers were at their highest, he felt himself to lie " under a cloud " ; not that this conviction had a repressive effect upon him. But on the whole, if we view the situation in its correct perspective, it does not appear that the " cloud " was as dense or as threatening as he imagined. The Pope never lost his memories of their meetings in Rome, when Newman was at Propaganda and at Santa Croce. " Personally," as Fr. Ryder says, " the late Pope had always treated him with kindness and consideration, and I know that Fr. Newman has always recognized this with gratitude." There was, however, a gulf between his former position and his later ; as an Anglican, he had been, within understood limits, a free-lance, whereas now, as a Catholic, he was a unit in a phalanx, retaining his own initiative, yet in his exercise of it subject to the scrutiny of authority ; and authority in the abstract, whatever the personal sentiments of those who wielded that authority, not understanding his peculiar position in England, was baffled by his general attitude and puzzled by the manner in which he recommended the Church to his countrymen. Nothing more clearly illustrates the official attitude towards him than the reception given in Rome to his famous *Letter to the Duke of Norfolk,* the classic of the almost forgotten controversy with Gladstone. Immediately upon its publication it was delated to Propaganda as containing censurable propositions. Thereupon Cardinal Franchi, the Prefect of Propaganda, wrote to Manning for his guidance on the most prudent line of action, and then notified Ullathorne, as Newman's Bishop, that the matter could not be ignored. Both, the former for no fewer than twelve reasons, urged caution, insisting upon the lamentable consequences that would result from a public censure. Yet, even so, after the lapse of eight months, Franchi instructed Ullathorne to draw Newman's attention, as though he were acting on his own initiative, to eleven propositions extracted from the pamphlet, as to which Abbot Butler remarks that "the reader . . . will probably be surprised at the kind of strictures on Popes deemed objectionable at Rome in 1875," [1] and to point out to him how injurious they might be, even against his intention, to others. Having had previous experience of the disadvantages of this method of indirect approach, Ullathorne urged Franchi to address himself to Newman "directly and openly." But what happened subsequently, remains obscure ; all that can be said, is that Newman seems to have been made cognizant of the incriminated propositions, since a copy of them is to be found among his papers. The most interesting document, however, is that in which Ullathorne discusses, as being the source of much misunderstanding, Newman's mode of argument, at once sympathetic and conciliatory, and sets it in contrast with the method, "more rigid than the schools," adopted by the "excessively dogmatic" W. G. Ward and his band of "zealots," which he dismisses as ineffective with enquirers, and disturbing to Catholics.[2] It is not likely, however, that his generous plea for toleration carried enough weight to win over the official mind. "It was not," as Abbot Butler pithily comments, "his line, but Manning's, that was wanted." [3]

Within four years the drama of Newman's life culminated in an unexpected climax. During that interval Pius IX had been removed from the scene by death, and with the accession of his successor a new spirit entered into the Papacy. Leo XIII, who had himself experienced the bitterness of lying " under a cloud," [1] heralded the dawn of a more tolerant day by conceiving a wish to raise Newman to the Sacred College in his first Consistory. " My Cardinal," he exclaimed years afterwards to Lord Selborne, who had come armed with a dutiful message from Newman, " it was not easy, it was not easy. They said he was too liberal ; but I had determined to honour the Church in honouring Newman. I always had a cult for him. I was proud that I was allowed to honour such a man." [2] To the recipient the signal honour bestowed upon him, in the circumstances a distinction almost without precedent, meant nothing in itself, for he had always prayed that he " might not rise to any ecclesiastical dignity " [3] ; he saw in it only the lifting of the cloud, the " thorough wiping away " of a " stigma," and the end of all the tittle-tattle that he was no more than " a half Catholic, a Liberal Catholic " ; it was " almost as though the heavens had opened, and the Divine voice had spoken its approval of him before the whole world." [4] In his *Biglietto* speech, which was a second *Apologia*, but addressed to a Catholic audience, he revealed what he conceived to have been his mission in life—the maintenance of dogmatic religion against the persistent erosion of Liberalism.

The posthumous volume, *Addresses and Replies*, bears witness to the ardour with which the personal devotion of the Catholics of these islands, suppressed through many years, at last found its voice ; but hardly less warm was the welcome given to the announcement of the Pope's intention among those outside the Church. Writing in the *Guardian*, Dean Church observed that there was " probably . . . not a single thing that the Pope could do which would be so heartily welcomed " [5] in England. That " the former Fellow of Oriel should . . . be surrounded with the pomp and state of a Cardinal " seemed to him extraordinary ; but more extraordinary still that the vicissitudes of life should have made of the " traitor " of 1845 " a man of whom Englishmen are so proud in 1879." [6] 1864 marked the

[1] At least Newman thought so, *W.*, II, 445.
[2] Butler, op. cit., II, 110.   [3] *W.*, I, 575.
[4] *Ibid.*, II, 445, 446, 452, 439.
[5] *Occasional Papers*, II, 465.   [6] *Ibid.*, II, 463.

turning-point between the ebb and flow of popular esteem ; and the *Apologia* must be regarded as the one effective cause of this revolution in public opinion. Can another single book in the history of literature be named that has wrought so amazing a change in its author's reputation ? The result was what he called a " wonderful deliverance." [1] " The kind feeling," he wrote on February 22, 1865, " was growing, when . . . I began the Kingsley controversy, the effect of which I need not enlarge on. . . . And thus I am in a totally different position now to what I was in January 1863. And my temptation at this moment is, to value the praise of men too highly, especially of Protestants—and to lose some portion of that sensitiveness towards God's praise which is so elementary a duty." [2] What the change amounted to, putting it at its lowest, was this, that he had, by his transparent sincerity, won the confidence of the public, which he had never before, even in his Tractarian days, completely possessed. As witness to this we may cite an Anglican correspondent, whom he quotes as having written to him in these terms : " You occupy a very unique position in England. There is no other man whose mere word would be more readily taken without the necessity of having it confirmed by any other testimony. I do not know any revolution of public feeling so complete as this." [3] It is a truly remarkable phenomenon that " one man at least has been held to be truly great by the nation, who has crossed all its prejudices and calmly ignored all its prepossessions " [4] ; and that this man, " the professed, the persistent denouncer of Liberalism, was welcomed back to his rightful place among Englishmen by none more warmly than by many Liberals." [5]

It was, as has been said, his sincerity that had first served to establish him in the good graces of his countrymen. " People could not resist the man who, after having so utterly discomfited his accuser, and vindicated himself by his strong right hand, proceeded to take them so simply and quietly into his confidence." [6] Before the controversy had gone very far, he

---

[1] *W.*, II, 72.   [2] *Ibid.*, II, 73.   [3] *W.*, II, 241.
[4] R. H. Hutton, *Cardinal Newman*, p. 1.
[5] Church, *Occasional Papers*, II, 465. It is alleged by F. Meyrick, *Memories*, p. 26, that Pusey in 1880 rebuked Newman for allowing the Oxford Liberals to play him " like a card."   [6] *Fr. Ryder*, MS.

fulfilled his own prophecy, " I will vanquish, not my Accuser, but my judges,"[1] and transformed them from judges into partizans. But even this is not enough to explain the remarkable hold he had upon the affections of his fellow-countrymen during the last two decades of his life.

In the *Apologia*, ignoring for the moment his maternal French ancestry, he roundly declared : " I had rather be an Englishman (as in fact I am,) than belong to any other race under heaven,"[2]—an Englishman to the backbone, " almost the unique cross between a true Briton of the proud school of Chatham and Burke, and the enthusiastic, devout, fervid Roman Catholic,"[3] but yet an Englishman, who saw and lamented the shortcomings of his country. It is only natural then that Dean Church should have found " the bond between him and his countrymen" in " his profound sympathy with the religiousness which still . . . marks England above all cultivated Christian nations."[4] When the distress entailed by the parting had lost its keenness, he recognised in the Anglican Church " a serviceable breakwater against doctrinal errors, more fundamental than its own,"[5] and in the ripeness of age he admitted his indebtedness to the Evangelical teachers of his youth.[6] In this connexion it will not be inapposite to recall here his close friendship with Dean Church, Lord Blachford, and Lord Coleridge, all Anglicans, who in 1879 acknowledged the great obligations to him under which they lay, to be " more than ever they can pay,"[7] his urbane intercourse with the non-conformist divines who sought him out, and his deep feeling for unbelievers such as the two younger Froudes, who may be taken as representative of the many others, men unknown even in their own generation, who came under his spell. From this sense of solidarity with his fellows came his lament in 1877, that " in our day Holy Church should present just that aspect to my countrymen which is most consonant with their ingrained prejudices against her, most unpromising for their conversion ; and what can one writer do to counteract this misfortune ? "[8]

---

[1] *Apo.*, p. xxii.   [2] p. xvi.
[3] *Life and Letters of Dean Church*, p. 270.
[4] *Occasional Papers*, II, 466.   [5] *Apo.*, p. 342.   [6] *W.*, II, 527.
[7] Coleridge, *Life of Lord Coleridge*, II, 280.   [8] *V.M.*, I, xxxvii.

His own influence was not enough. Fr. Ryder explains why :
" Ever since the publication of the *Apologia*, Cardinal Newman
has been accepted by the general public . . . as . . . an
Englishman with his heart in the right place—no ' Inglese
Italianato,' as the old phrase went, but one in whose affections
his country and his countrymen had never ceased to hold their
own. Thus it often happened that persons who could not find
a civil word to say of the Pope or of aught to him appertaining,
always made an exception in favour of Fr. Newman, adding,
more frequently than not, that of course he did not count,
seeing that he was in his present position a kind of *lusus naturae*,
an exception proving the rule." [1]

One national English trait he has called attention to in the
character of Hurrell Froude, of whom he says that combined
with " a keen insight into abstract truth," he displayed a " severe
adherence to the real and the concrete." [2] He might with equal
truth have made the same remark about himself. In fact, he
did admit that his " turn of mind " had been " logical, ethical,
practical," rather than metaphysical,[3] and that perhaps comes
to the same thing. He was always intensely conscious of " that
imperfection, which must ever attend the abstract, when it
would determine the concrete," [4] especially in matters of human
psychology. The title of one of his more famous sermons,
The Individuality of the Soul,[5] enunciates the principle that guided
him in his relations with his fellows. The individual man is
real in a sense in which the genus *homo* is not ; his thought
and his action are conditioned, not by humanity in the
abstract, but by men, individual men, in the concrete, each
man with " his own individuality, his separate history, his
antecedents and his future, his duties, his responsibilities, his
solemn trial, and his eternity." [6] Men responded to that personal approach, and felt it even in his sermons. " He seemed,"
says J. A. Froude of the then distant Sunday afternoons in St.
Mary's, " to be addressing the most secret consciousness of each
of us—as the eyes of a portrait appear to look at every person
in a room." [7] It was his keen sensitiveness to the claims of the

[1] *W.*, II, 358.   [2] *Apo.*, p. 24.   [3] *S.E.*, p. 94.
[4] *Idea*, p. 52.   [5] *P.S.*, IV, 80–93.   [6] *A.R.*, p. 307.
[7] *Short Studies, etc.* (1894), IV, 283. Cf. *Nemesis of Faith* (Scott Library), p. 157.

individual for understanding and sympathy, and his perception of the only effective manner of satisfying those claims, that made him, enlarging the reference in a phrase from St. Francis of Sales, choose for his motto the words : " *Cor ad cor loquitur.*" [1]

In his *Discours* on the occasion of his reception into the French Academy, M. André Bellessort, said of his predecessor, the Abbé Bremond, that in Newman he had found one who was " at once his brother and his hero." How many in his lifetime would have re-echoed the sentiment expressed in these words, even though they would have preferred to speak of him as " the Father of their Souls." His apostolate among them was carried on, partly through personal interviews, but mainly through correspondence. " La poste," as Bremond picturesquely puts it, " ne chômait guère entre Edgbaston et tous les points du Royaume-Uni." [2] Diverse were the subjects on which he was consulted by correspondents known or unknown to him ; and he put himself at the service of all without distinction. Those who lived with him, have borne their witness to the strange phenomenon of a Roman Cardinal acting as spiritual adviser to Protestant England, and helping in their difficulties, intellectual or spiritual, members of various religious bodies who showed no leaning towards Catholicism. But the fruits of this apostolate can hardly be estimated. The fact that it was being patiently carried on, was known to his immediate circle ; but the details would naturally have remained a secret between himself and his correspondents, unless they chose to reveal their part in it.

He read the signs of the times in the steady drift towards Liberalism—a Liberalism indebted to the " movement of which he was the soul " for its " largeness of mind and warmth," and so far forth diverse from the " dry, repulsive, narrow, material Liberalism of the Reform era " [3]—which was " sweeping into its own ranks great numbers of able, earnest, virtuous men, elderly men of approved antecedents, young men with a career before them." [4] With this portent before his eyes, too manifest to be ignored, he wrote in 1877 : " As to the prospects of the

---

[1] *Œuvres*, XII, 321, Le cœur parle au cœur. Cf. *Idea*, p. 410.
[2] *Newman*, p. xxv.
[3] Church, *Occasional Papers*, II, 396. [4] *W.*, II, 462.

Church, . . . you know old men are generally desponding—
but my apprehensions are not new, but above 50 years standing,
I have all that time thought that a time of wide-spread infidelity
was coming, and through all those years the waters have in fact
been rising as a deluge. I look for the time, after my life, when
only the tops of the mountains will be seen like islands in the
waste of waters. I speak principally of the Protestant world
—but great actions and successes must be achieved by the
Catholic leaders, great wisdom as well as courage must be given
them from on high, if Holy Church is to be kept safe from this
awful calamity, and, though any trial which came upon her
would but be temporary, it may be fierce in the extreme
while it lasts." [1] Recurring to the same subject a few months
later, he brought out how complete was the revolution that
had taken place in the general attitude towards religion in the
course of a few years : " The spread of scepticism is portentous
—and the great mischief is that there is a general antecedent
leaning to the side of unbelief, as the more reasonable and
probable. A notion prevails that great changes are coming,
so that men believe atheism before they have discovered
revelation." [2]

Scepticism he likened to an " epidemic," an epidemic
" wonderfully catching " ; and he considered the imagination,
not the intellect, to be the seat of the infection. " The
imagination," he explained in 1882, " presents a possible,
plausible view of things which haunts and at length overcomes
the mind. We begin by asking " How can we be sure that it
is not so ? " and this thought hides from the mind the real
rational grounds on which our faith is founded. Then our
faith goes, and how in the world is it ever to be regained,
except by a wonderful grant of God's grace. May God keep
us all from this terrible deceit of the latter days. What is
coming upon us ? I look with keen compassion on the next
generation and with, I may say, awe." [3] Indeed, with apprehension, as well as with awe, for the sight of " clever and
thoughtful " young men raised in his mind the question, how
will they " be able to stand against the intellectual flood . . .
setting in against Christianity " ? [4]

[1] W., II. 416.   [2] Ibid., II, 416.   [3] Ibid., II, 478.   [4] Ibid., II, 474.

The opening years of the new Pontificate were years of promise destined to bear their fruit in due season. The intransigent attitude adopted by Pius IX in face of the welter of international politics was discarded by his successor, who for more than thirty years had shown an alert and independent mind in the administration of his diocese of Perugia, and now in a more exalted sphere gave evidence of an equally enlightened outlook in regard to larger problems and wider issues. The subject of education came to the front ; and this being his particular " line," Newman felt that he could speak with a certain authority. Assured of a sympathetic ear in the Vatican, and confident that his words, as Cardinal, would now carry greater weight, he seized the opportunity, in spite of his age and his infirmities, to make his views known. Thus, on the appearance of the Encyclical, *Aeterni Patris* (August 4, 1879), which inaugurated the general revival of the *philosophia perennis* according to the mind of St. Thomas Aquinas, he wrote, and perhaps sent to the Pope, a letter, in which, after adverting to the " first necessity," that the intellectual life of the Church should be " founded upon broad as well as true principles," and theological speculation " grafted on the Catholic tradition of philosophy," as mediated through the four great doctors, Athanasius, Augustine, Anselm, and Aquinas, he expressed his entire agreement with the Encyclical, as apposite to " a time when there is so much cultivation of mind, so much intellectual excitement, so many new views, true and false, and so much temptation to overstep the old truth." [1]

After his return from Rome in 1879, he contemplated the project of translating into Latin selected portions of his own writings, being confident that, if his views were correctly presented, they would not " be found in substance to disagree with St. Thomas," [2] and he even made some tentative experiments in that direction ; but he had left it too late, and they were discontinued. Having, however, become personally acquainted in Rome with certain eminent theologians who shared his desire to quicken the intellectual life of the Church, he fully intended, when his health permitted, to repeat his

[1] *W.*, II, 501–2.
[2] From a letter to R. Whitty, S.J., December 20. 1878.

visit, " looking forward to talking with some who had not followed him in all his writings, and to becoming conversant with many matters of interest and importance. Moreover, and above all things, he desired to open his mind fully to the Holy Father on those educational subjects which had occupied him so much, and concerning which his knowledge and experience were exceptional." [1] But the weight of years frustrated that cherished design. One day, however, in conversation with Fr. Neville, he confided to him what, if he were in the Pope's place, he would do. His own life would be too short to achieve much, but he would " appoint and organise commissions on various subjects, and thus advance work for another to take up if he willed," on the basis of the full and candid reports, which would be demanded from them ; and he specified in particular, as subjects demanding special attention, Biblical Criticism and early Church History. [2]

His physical frailty occasioned in him intense regret, when he learnt in 1882 that representations were to be made in Rome against the ban prohibiting the frequentation of the English Universities by Catholics. Unable to do more, he wrote a letter in which he recalled his own endeavours and their frustration : " It is for years beyond numbering—in one view of the matter for these fifty years—that I have been crying out : " I have laboured in vain ; I have spent my strength without cause, and in vain ; wherefore my judgment is with the Lord and my work with my God." Now at the end of my days, when the next world is close upon me, I am recognised at last at Rome. Don't suppose I am dreaming of complaint ; just the contrary. The Prophet's words which expressed my keen pain, brought, because they were his words, my consolation. It is the rule of God's Providence, that we should succeed by failure." [3] A few days later he supplemented this in a second letter, which was laid before the Pope in an Italian translation. In it he expressed his views forcibly on the Oxford question, which seemed to him " the cardinal question for the moment." " The under-graduates and Junior Fellows," he wrote, " are sheep without a shepherd. They are sceptics or inquirers, quite open for

---

[1] Fr. Neville, quoted in *W.*, II, 476.
[2] *Ibid.*, II, 477.   [3] *Ibid.*, II, 485.

religious influences. . . . But is it not heart piercing that such an opportunity should be lost ? The Liberals are sweeping along in triumph, without any Catholic or religious influence to stem them. . . . This is what I feel at the moment, but, alas, it is only one out of various manifestations of what may be called Nihilism in the Catholic Body, and in its rulers. They forbid, but they do not direct or create." [1] The Pope was impressed by this clear view of the situation, and promised to lay it before Manning ; but whatever effect Newman's intervention may have had, it was not until 1895, when both Manning and Newman had passed from this earthly scene, that the ban was at last lifted.

Newman's final views on the subject which had, throughout his long life, lain as a heavy burden upon his mind, but had no less served as a stimulus to his thought, have been put on record by the devoted piety of Wilfrid Ward, who owed his formation in a large sense to Newman, and happily sought to discharge his debt by his tireless efforts to ensure that the intellectual heritage left to Catholics by his master, at once his father's friend and victim, should not die out of their memory, as though he were no more than a Victorian thinker with a message addressed to his own age, but no longer relevant. The pages which contain his synoptic review of their last conversations [2] it would be undiscerning to disregard ; they may be, as their writer admits, merely an appendix to Newman's published works, but they have an independent value, since they throw into relief the supreme object, which unified and controlled all his divergent activities. They cannot easily be epitomised without loss ; but it may be well to draw attention to his two practical suggestions to meet the needs of the two classes of men in whom he was mainly interested—inquiring minds outside the Church struggling against the drift towards agnosticism, and active minds within the Church sensitive to the advance of contemporary science : viz., encouragement of specialized research among Catholics, and toleration of free discussion between theologians and scientists within the limits of their respective fields of study. Lastly, " he dreaded the decay of theology, which must come, if theologians ceased to be

[1] *W.*, II, 486.   [2] *Ibid.*, II, 490 ff.

genuine thinkers . . . and became merely, as it were, lawyers well versed in precedent, who recorded what the schools had or had not regarded as obligatory, forgetting that the *data* of many problems had now changed and the weight of evidence accordingly shifted. It was active thought which he desiderated among them—not a change of theological principles, but their more intelligent application. And he regarded specialists as the only trustworthy witnesses as to where modification was really necessary in the existing teaching." [1]

" The visible Church, with its unbroken tradition, appealed alike to the imagination and the reason as bearing witness to religious truth against the unbelieving world." [2] As the latter has changed its methods of assault from age to age, so it is ever incumbent on the former to adopt the appropriate counter-measures. This is what gives individuals their importance in the ecclesiastical body politic ; since it is they who always " have taken the initiative, and given the lead to the Catholic mind, in theological inquiry." [3] The active mind is no less active within the Church than without ; but the Church, as " the pillar and ground of the truth," serves as a " sort of *remora*," [4] a curb upon the excesses into which the active mind is prone to run. In spite of all his pleas for freedom of thought, for candour and fairness, Newman never minimized the deference, the submission, due to authority, not only in the abstract, but in the concrete. Just as he had said that his Bishop in his Anglican days was his Pope,[5] so afterwards, even in moments of the utmost stress, he would have said without reserve that the Pope was the Vicar of Christ ; and for him that would have been the end of the matter. " It is the custom with Protestant writers to consider that, whereas there are two great principles in action in the history of religion, Authority and Private Judgment, they have all the Private Judgment to themselves, and we have the full inheritance and the super-incumbent oppression of Authority. But this is not so ; it is the vast Catholic body itself, and it only, which affords an arena for both combatants in that awful, never-dying duel. It is necessary for the very life of religion, viewed in its large

[1] *W.*, II, 498–9.   [2] *Ibid.*, II, 498.
[3] *Apo.*, p. 265.   [4] *Ibid.*   [5] *Ibid.*, p. 51.

operations and its history, that the warfare should be incessantly carried on. Every exercise of Infallibility is brought out into act by an intense and varied operation of the Reason, both as its ally and as its opponent, and provokes again, when it has done its work, a re-action of Reason against it ; and, as in a civil polity the State exists and endures by means of the rivalry and collision, the encroachments and defeats of its constituent parts, so in like manner Catholic Christendom is no simple exhibition of religious absolutism, but presents a continuous picture of Authority and Private Judgment alternately advancing and retreating in the ebb and flow of the tide ;—it is a vast assemblage of human beings with wilful intellects and wild passions, brought together into one by the beauty and the Majesty of a Superhuman Power,—into what may be called a large reformatory, or training-school, not as if into a hospital or into a prison, not in order to be sent to bed, not to be buried alive, but (if I may change my metaphor) brought together as if into some moral factory, for the melting, refining, and moulding, by an incessant, noisy, process, of the raw material of human nature, so excellent, so dangerous, so capable of divine purposes." [1]

"I shall cheerfully leave it to time to do for me what Time has so often done. . . . Time has been my best friend and champion ; and to the future I lovingly commit myself with much resignation to its award." [2] In these terms Newman replied to John Morley's invitation to him to answer Leslie Stephen's criticisms in the *Fortnightly Review*. On this note, wrung from him by an acute sense of his " present discontents " tempered by the deep assurance that, " if only we are patient, God works for us," this introduction to his " living thoughts " may fitly end. But how " living " ? A thinker's place in the scale of values depends upon the relevance of his thought to the generations, as they come and go in endless succession. Can it be said that Newman lost his significance, when his generation passed away ? That is a large question, and one that cannot be answered summarily, or from a single angle. Bishop Hedley has stated his claims upon the present and the future more comprehensively and aptly than many another writer : " As

[1] *Apo.*, p. 252.   [2] Quoted from the rough draft.

the years pass . . . Newman's greatness will grow in the minds of men. For his greatness rests on his having seen some of the most vital truths that can affect human destiny, and expressed them in a language that is perfect and absolute. When a man who has this gift of vision and this perfection of expression is also a soul that is united with his God and a character so winning that men are drawn to love him, his name is secure, and it will pass into the company of the world's greatest." [1] The one subject that furnished the core of his thought, will exercise the minds of every succeeding generation, because it raises the eternal problems, problems that will demand and receive answers, as long as mankind continues in its present state of probation.

For this actual generation, not to look further forward, of Catholics at least, in every country, his writings have a peculiar interest, since he anticipated and forecast, through his insight into the latent tendencies of thought in his own age, what their *dénouement* would be in the next. Hence there is a prophetic strain discernible in all his utterances. Fr. Przywara, the eminent German Catholic philosopher, who is also a singularly discriminating and balanced exponent of Newman, associates St. Augustine and St. Thomas with him, as representatives of their epochs at their culminating points, the ancient, the medieval, and the modern respectively, all three sharing in the autumnal mellowness of age, typified by Moses " upon Mount Nebo," contemplating " all the land of Galaad, as far as Dan," stretched out before him.[2] But Newman is more nearly akin to St. Augustine than to St. Thomas, not only in the fashion of his thought, but in the psychological environment of his life. " It was," as Fr. Przywara has elsewhere written, " in presence of the fall of the old world that Augustine rose to this ultimate and most sublime vision. Newman saw man, the world, and history from the already almost prophetic perspective revealed to him by that final struggle between Christ and anti-Christ legible on the countenance of the modern world. He is thus the peculiar and unique *Augustinus redivivus* of modern times, and that because, amidst the torrent which

[1] *Ampleforth Journal,* April 1912.
[2] Deut. xxxiv. *Religionsphilosophie Katholischer Theologie,* p. 82.

bears all things to their doom, his gaze is calmly fixed upon the God of the end. DEUS *omnia in omnibus*." [1] He foresaw the inescapable consequences involved in the triumph of Liberalism—the decay of belief, the lowering of moral standards, uncertainty about man's destiny, and despair ; but he could not, even in a nightmare fantastic beyond conception, have anticipated the horror of which we have been the living witnesses. How could he have guessed what our grim experience has taught us, that the barbarism of a degenerate civilization, with all the devices of modern science at its command, may sink to far lower depths of degradation than the barbarism of a world as yet uncivilized ?

A century and more ago, when the peace of Oxford reflected the peace of England, of the world, he called upon his hearers, in prospect of the persecution of Antichrist, to be, as " Christians in heart" should be, "pilgrims, watchers waiting for the morning, waiting for the light, straining [their] eyes for the first dawn of day." [2] As in the successive phases of his own life, so, too, in the processes of history, he discerned the agency of God, overruling, controlling, directing events towards the fulfilment of the Divine Purpose. "I have ever anticipated," he said in what is perhaps his last letter [3] on the subject, " a great battle between good and evil, and have ever been led to think the duty of the champions of truth, when the conflict came, was anticipated for them in the words of Moses : 'Fear ye not ; stand still and see *Magnalia Dei*. He shall fight for you, and ye shall hold your peace.' " [4] We have seen the battle joined, and the first phase fought to a conclusion. The end is not yet ; but when that end comes, it will be, not as men may fear or hope, but as God wills.

[1] *A Monument to St. Augustine*, p. 286. [2] *D.A.*, p. 106.
[3] Dated May 17, 1883. [4] Ex. xiv, 13–14.

THE PRINCIPAL WORKS OF

CARDINAL NEWMAN

(1801–1890)

St. Bartholomew's Eve : a tale of the sixteenth century (with J. W. Bowden) (1821)

The Arians of the fourth century (1833)

Five Letters on Church Reform (1833)

Tracts for the Times (contributor) (1833–41)

Lyra Apostolica (1836)

Elucidations of Dr. Hampden's Theological Statements (1836)

Letter to the Margaret Professor of Divinity (1838)

Lectures on the Prophetical Office of the Church (1837)

Parochial Sermons, 1834–42

Lectures on Justification (1838)

The Church of the Fathers, 1840

A Letter to Richard (Bagot), Bishop of Oxford (1841)

Sermons on Subjects of the Day (1843)

Plain Sermons V (1843)

Sermons before the University of Oxford (1843)

Select Treatise of St. Athanasius, trans. with notes (1842–4)

Lives of St. Bettelin (prose only), St. Edelwald and St. Gundleus in Lives of the English Saints (1844)

An Essay on the Development of Christian Doctrine (1845)

Loss and Gain (1848)

Discourses addressed to Mixed Congregations (1849)

Lectures on certain Difficulties felt by Anglicans (1850)

Lectures on the Present Position of Catholics in England (1851)

Discourses on the Scope and Nature of University Education (1852)

Verses on Religious Subjects (1853)

Lectures on the History of the Turks in its relation to Christianity (1854)

Callista : a Sketch of the Third Century (1856)

The Office and Work of Universities (1856)

Sermons preached on various occasions (1857)

Lectures and Essays on University Subjects (1859)

Mr. Kingsley and Dr. Newman : a Correspondence (1864)

Apologia pro Vita Sua (1864)

A Letter to the Rev. E. B. Pusey (1866)

The Dream of Gerontius (1866)

Verses on Various Occasions (1868)

An Essay in aid of a Grammar of Assent (1870)

Causes of the Rise and Success of Arianism (1872)

The Heresy of Apollinaris (1874)

A Letter addressed to His Grace the Duke of Norfolk (1875)

Stray Essays on Controversial Points (1890)

Meditations and Devotions (1893)

The following volumes in the Uniform Edition, edited by Newman himself (1869–1881), contain articles contributed to periodicals or papers originally published as pamphlets :

Two Essays on Miracles (1870)

Essays Critical and Historical (1871)

Historical Sketches (1872)

Discussions and Arguments (1872)

The Idea of a University (1873)

Tracts Theological and Ecclesiastical (1874)

The Via Media (1877)

THE INTELLECTUAL HERESY OF THE AGE

To his Mother

March 13, 1829.

WHAT A SCRIBBLER I AM BECOME ! BUT THE FACT IS MY mind is so full of ideas, in consequence of this important event, and my views have so much enlarged and expanded, that in justice to myself I ought to write a volume.

We live in a novel era—one in which there is an advance towards universal education. Men have hitherto depended on others, and especially on the clergy, for religious truth ; now each man attempts to judge for himself. Now, without meaning of course that Christianity is in itself opposed to free inquiry, still I think it *in fact* at the present time opposed to the particular form which that liberty of thought has now assumed. Christianity is of faith, modesty, lowliness, subordination ; but the spirit at work against it is one of latitudinarianism, indifferentism, republicanism, and schism, a spirit which tends to overthrow doctrine, as if the fruit of bigotry and discipline, as if the instrument of priestcraft. All parties seem to acknowledge that the stream of opinion is setting against the Church. I do believe it will ultimately be separated from the State, and at this prospect I look with apprehension : 1. because all revolutions are awful things, and the effect of this revolution is unknown ; 2. because the upper classes will be left almost religionless ; 3. because there will not be that security for sound doctrine without change, which is given by Act of Parliament ; 4. because the clergy will be thrown on their congregations for voluntary contributions.

It is no reply to say that the majesty of truth will triumph, for man's nature is corrupt. Also, even should it triumph, still this will only be ultimately, and the meanwhile may last for centuries. Yet I do still think there is a promise of preservation to the Church, and in its Sacraments preceding and attending religious education there are such means of heavenly grace, that I do not doubt it will live on in the most irreligious and atheistical times.

Its enemies at present are : 1. the uneducated or partially educated mass in towns, whose organs are Wooler's, Carlisle's publications, etc. They are almost professedly deistical or worse. 2. The Utilitarians, political economists, useful knowledge people ; their organs the *Westminster Review*, the London University. 3. The schismatics, in and out of the Church, whose organs are the *Eclectic Review*, the *Christian Guardian*, etc. 4. The Baptists, whose system is consistent Calvinism, for, as far as I can see, Thomas Scott, etc., are inconsistent, and such inconsistent men would in times of commotion split, and go over to this side or that. 5. The high circles in London. 6. I might add the political indifferentists, but I do not know enough to speak, like men who join Roman Catholics on one hand and Socinians on the other. Now you must not understand me as speaking harshly of individuals ; I am speaking of bodies and principles.

And now I come to another phenomenon : the talent of the day is against the Church. The Church party (visibly at least, for there may be latent talent, and great times give birth to great men) is poor in mental endowments. It has not activity, shrewdness, dexterity, eloquence, practical power. On what then does it depend ? On prejudice and bigotry.

This is hardly an exaggeration ; yet I have good meaning and one honourable to the Church. Listen to my theory. As each individual has certain instincts of right and wrong, antecedently to reasoning, on which he acts and rightly so, which perverse reasoning may supplant, which then can hardly be regained, but, if regained, will be regained from a different source, from reasoning, not from nature, so, I think, has the world of men collectively. God gave them truths in His miraculous revelations, and other truths, in the unsophisticated infancy of nations, scarcely less necessary and divine. These are transmitted as " the wisdom of our ancestors," through men, many of whom cannot enter into them, or receive them themselves, still on, on, from age to age, not the less truths, because many of the generations, through which they are transmitted, are unable to prove them, but hold them either from pious and honest feeling (it may be) or from bigotry or from prejudice. That they are truths, it is most difficult to prove ; for great men alone can prove great ideas or grasp them. Such a mind was Hooker's, such Butler's ; and, as moral evil triumphs over good on a small field of action, so in the argument of an hour, or the compass of a volume, would men like Brougham, or again Wesley, show to far greater advantage than Hooker or Butler. Moral truth is gained by patient study, by calm reflection, silently as the dew falls, unless miraculously given ; and, when gained, it is transmitted by faith and by "prejudice." Keble's book is full of such truths ; which any Cambridge man might refute with the greatest ease.

Letters and Correspondence

I would say this then :—that a system of doctrine has risen up during the last three centuries, in which faith or spiritual-mindedness is contemplated and rested on as the end of religion instead of Christ. I do not mean to say that Christ is not mentioned as the Author of all good, but that stress is laid rather on the believing than on the Object of belief, on the comfort and persuasiveness of the doctrine rather than on the doctrine itself. And in this way religion is made to consist in contemplating ourselves instead of Christ ; not simply in looking to Christ, but in ascertaining that we look to Christ, not in His Divinity and Atonement, but in our conversion and our faith in those truths.

Of course nothing is more natural or suitable than for a Christian to describe and dwell on the difference between one who believes and one who does not believe. The fault here spoken of is the giving to our " experiences " a more prominent place in our thoughts than to the nature, attributes, and work of Him from whom they profess to come,—the insisting on them as a special point for the consideration of all who desire to be recognized as converted and elect. When men are to be exhorted to newness of life, the true Object to be put before them, as I conceive, is " Jesus Christ, the same yesterday, to-day, and for ever " ; the true Gospel preaching is to enlarge, as they can bear it, on the Person, natures, attributes, offices, and work of Him who once regenerated them, and is now ready to pardon ; to dwell upon His recorded words and deeds on earth ; to declare reverently and adoringly His mysterious greatness as the Only-begotten Son, One with the Father, yet distinct from Him ; of Him, yet not apart from Him ; eternal, yet begotten ; a Son, yet as if a servant ; and to combine and to contrast His attributes and relations to us as God and man, as our Mediator, Saviour, Sanctifier, and Judge. The true preaching of the Gospel is to preach Christ. But the fashion of the day has been, instead of this, to preach conversion ; to attempt to convert by insisting on conversion ; to exhort men to undergo a change ; to tell them to be sure they look at Christ, instead of simply holding up Christ to them ; to tell them to have faith, rather than to supply its Object ; to lead them to stir up and work up their minds, instead of impressing on them the thought of Him who can savingly work in them ; to bid them take care that their faith is justifying, not dead, formal, self-righteous, and merely moral, whereas the image of Christ fully delineated of itself destroys deadness, formality, and self-righteousness ; to rely on words, vehemence, eloquence, and the like, rather than to aim at conveying the one great evangelical idea whether in words or not. And thus faith and (what is called) spiritual-mindedness are dwelt on as *ends,* and obstruct the view of Christ, just as the Law was perverted by the Jews.

* * *

Poor miserable captives, to whom such doctrine is preached as the Gospel ! What ! is *this* the liberty wherewith Christ has made us free, and wherein we stand, the home of our own thoughts, the prison of our own sensations, the province of self, a monotonous confession of what we are by nature, not what Christ is in us, and a resting at best not on His love towards us, but in our faith towards Him ! This is nothing but a specious idolatry ; a man thus minded does not simply think of God when he prays to Him, but is observing whether he feels properly or not ; does not believe and obey, but considers it enough to be conscious that he is what he calls warm and spiritual ; does not contemplate the grace of the Blessed Eucharist, the Body and Blood of His Saviour Christ, except— O shameful and fearful error !—except as a quality of his own mind.

* * *

And this being the difference between true faith and self-contemplation, no wonder that where the thought of self obscures the thought of God, prayer and praise languish, and only preaching flourishes. Divine worship is simply contemplating our Maker, Redeemer, Sanctifier, and Judge ; but discoursing, conversing, making speeches, arguing, reading, and writing about religion, tend to make us forget Him in ourselves. The Ancients worshipped ; they went out of their own minds into the Infinite Temple which was around them. They saw Christ in the Gospels, in the Creed, in the Sacraments and other Rites ; in the visible structure and ornaments of His House, in the Altar, and in the Cross ; and, not content with giving the service of their eyes, they gave Him their voices, their bodies, and their time, gave up their rest by night and their leisure by day, all that could evidence the offering of their hearts to Him. . . . Unwavering, unflagging, not urged by fits and starts, not heralding forth their feelings, but resolutely, simply, perseveringly, day after day, Sunday and week-day, fast-day and festival, week by week, season by season, year by year, in youth and in age, through a life, thirty years, forty years, fifty years, in prelude of the everlasting chant before the Throne,—so they went on, " continuing *instant* in prayer," after the pattern of Psalmists and Apostles, in the day with David, in the night with Paul and Silas, winter and summer, in heat and in cold, in peace and in danger, in a prison or in a cathedral, in the dark, in the day-break, at sun-rising, in the forenoon, at noon, in the afternoon, at eventide, and on going to rest, still they had Christ before them ; His thought in their mind, His emblems in their eye, His name in their mouth, His service in their posture, magnifying Him, and calling on all that lives to magnify Him, joining with Angels in heaven and Saints in Paradise to bless and praise Him for ever and ever. . . . To look to Christ is to be justified by faith ; to think of being justified by faith is to look from Christ and to fall from grace.

Lectures on Justification

THE IMMINENT PERIL OF THE CHURCH

While I was engaged in writing my work upon the Arians, great events were happening at home and abroad, which brought out into form and passionate expression the various beliefs which had so gradually been winning their way into my mind. Shortly before, there had been a Revolution in France; the Bourbons had been dismissed: and I held that it was unchristian for nations to cast off their governors, and, much more, sovereigns who had the divine right of inheritance. Again, the great Reform Agitation was going on around me as I wrote. The Whigs had come into power; Lord Grey had told the Bishops to set their house in order, and some of the Prelates had been insulted and threatened in the streets of London. The vital question was, how were we to keep the Church from being liberalized? there was such apathy on the subject in some quarters, such imbecile alarm in others; the true principles of Churchmanship seemed so radically decayed, and there was such distraction in the councils of the Clergy. Blomfield, the Bishop of London of the day, an active and open-hearted man, had been for years engaged in diluting the high orthodoxy of the Church by the introduction of members of the Evangelical body into places of influence and trust. He had deeply offended men who agreed in opinion with myself, by an off-hand saying (as it was reported) to the effect that belief in the Apostolical succession had gone out with the Non-jurors. "We can count you," he said to some of the gravest and most venerated persons of the old school. And the Evangelical party itself, with their late successes, seemed to have lost that simplicity and unworldliness which I admired so much in Milner and Scott. It was not that I did not venerate such men as Ryder, the then Bishop of Lichfield, and others of similar sentiments, who were not yet promoted out of the ranks of the Clergy, but I thought little of the Evangelicals as a class. I thought they played into the hands of the Liberals. With the Establishment thus divided and threatened, thus ignorant of its true strength, I compared that fresh vigorous

48

Power of which I was reading in the first centuries. In her triumphant zeal on behalf of the Primeval Mystery, to which I had had so great a devotion from my youth, I recognized the movement of my Spiritual Mother. " Incessu patuit Dea." The self-conquest of her Ascetics, the patience of her Martyrs, the irresistible determination of her Bishops, the joyous swing of her advance, both exalted and abashed me. I said to myself, " Look on this picture and on that " ; I felt affection for my own Church, but not tenderness ; I felt dismay at her prospects, anger and scorn at her do-nothing perplexity. I thought that if Liberalism once got a footing within her, it was sure of the victory in the event. I saw that Reformation principles were powerless to rescue her. As to leaving her, the thought never crossed my imagination ; still I ever kept before me that there was something greater than the Established Church, and that that was the Church Catholic and Apostolic, set up from the beginning, of which she was but the local presence and the organ. She was nothing, unless she was this. She must be dealt with strongly, or she would be lost. There was need of a second reformation.

* * *

[The Froudes and I] set out in December, 1832. . . . I went to various coasts of the Mediterranean ; parted with my friends at Rome ; went down for the second time to Sicily without companion, at the end of April ; and got back to England by Palermo in the early part of July. . . . My general feeling was, " All, save the spirit of man, is divine." I saw nothing but what was external ; of the hidden life of Catholics I knew nothing. I was still more driven back into myself, and felt my isolation. England was in my thoughts solely, and the news from England came rarely and imperfectly. The Bill for the Suppression of the Irish Sees was in progress, and filled my mind. I had fierce thoughts against the Liberals.

* * *

It was at Rome . . . that we began the *Lyra Apostolica* which appeared monthly in the *British Magazine*. The motto shows the feeling of both Froude and myself at the time : we borrowed from M. Bunsen a Homer, and Froude chose the words in which Achilles, on returning to the battle, says, " You shall know the difference, now that I am back again."

Especially when I was left by myself, the thought came upon me that deliverance is wrought, not by the many but by the few, not by bodies but by persons. Now it was, I think, that I repeated to myself the words, which had ever been dear to me from my school days, " Exoriare aliquis ! "—now too, that Southey's beautiful poem of Thalaba, for which I had an immense liking, came forcibly to my mind. I began to think that I had a mission. There are sentences of my letters to my friends to this effect, if they are not destroyed. When we took leave of Monsignore Wiseman, he had courteously expressed a wish that we might' make a second visit to Rome ; I said with great gravity, " We have a work to do in England." I went down at once to Sicily, and the presentiment grew stronger. I struck into the middle of the island, and fell ill of a fever at Leonforte. My servant thought that I was dying, and begged for my last directions. I gave them, as he wished ; but I said, " I shall not die." I repeated, " I shall not die, for I have not sinned against light, I have not sinned against light." I never have been able quite to make out what I meant. . . . My servant, who had acted as my nurse, asked what ailed me. I could only answer him, " I have a work to do in England."

I was aching to get home. . . . At last I got off again, and did not stop night or day, (except a compulsory delay at Paris,) till I reached England, and my mother's house. . . . This was on the Tuesday. The following Sunday, July 14th, Mr. Keble preached the Assize Sermon in the University Pulpit. . . . I have ever considered and kept the day, as the start of the religious movement of 1833.

Apologia

THE CALL TO ARMS

A

Living movements do not come of committees, nor are great ideas worked out through the post, even though it had been the penny post. This principle deeply penetrated both Froude and myself from the first, and recommended to us the course which things soon took spontaneously, and without set purpose of our own. . . . I, on the other hand, had out of my own head begun the Tracts; and these, as representing the antagonist principle of personality, were looked upon by Mr. Palmer's friends with considerable alarm. . . . Mr. Perceval wrote to me in support of the judgment of Mr. Palmer and the dignitaries. I replied in a letter, which he afterwards published. " As to the Tracts," I said to him (I quote my own words from his Pamphlet), " every one has his own taste. You object to some things, another to others. If we altered to please every one, the whole effect would be spoiled. They were not intended as symbols *è cathedrâ,* but as the expression of individual minds; and individuals, feeling strongly, while on the one hand, they are incidentally faulty in mode or language, are still peculiarly effective. No great work was done by a system; whereas systems rise out of individual exertions. Luther was an individual. The very faults of an individual excite attention; he loses, but his cause (if good and he powerful-minded) gains. This is the way of things; we promote truth by a self-sacrifice."

Apologia

★ ★ ★

B

THOUGHTS ON THE MINISTERIAL COMMISSION

Respectfully addressed to the Clergy

I am but one of yourselves,—a Presbyter; and therefore I conceal my name, lest I should take too much on myself by speaking in my own person. Yet speak I must ; for the times are very evil, yet no one speaks against them.

Is not this so ? Do not we "look upon one another," yet perform nothing ? Do we not all confess the peril into which the Church is come, yet sit still each in his own retirement, as if mountains and seas cut off brother from brother ? Therefore suffer me, while I try to draw you forth from those pleasant retreats, which it has been our blessedness hitherto to enjoy, to contemplate the condition and prospects of our Holy Mother in a practical way ; so that one and all may unlearn that idle habit, which has grown upon us, of owning the state of things to be bad, yet doing nothing to remedy it.

Consider a moment. Is it fair, is it dutiful, to suffer our Bishops to stand the brunt of the battle without doing our part to support them ? Upon them comes "the care of all the Churches." This cannot be helped ; indeed it is their glory. Not one of us would wish in the least to deprive them of the duties, the toils, the responsibilities of their high Office. And, black event as it would be for the country, yet, (as far as they are concerned,) we could not wish them a more blessed termination of their course, than the spoiling of their goods, and martyrdom.

To them then we willingly and affectionately relinquish their high privileges and honors ; we encroach not upon the rights of the SUCCESSORS OF THE APOSTLES ; we touch not their sword and crosier. Yet surely we may be their shield-bearers in the battle without offence ; and by our voice and deeds be to them what Luke and Timothy were to St. Paul.

Now then let me come at once to the subject which leads me to address you. Should the Government and Country so far forget their God as to cast off the Church, to deprive it of its temporal honors and substance, *on what* will you rest the claim of respect and attention which you make upon your flocks ? Hitherto you have been upheld by your birth, your education, your wealth, your connexions ; should these secular advantages cease, on what must Christ's Ministers depend ? Is not this a serious practical question ? We know how miserable is the state of religious bodies not supported by the State. Look at the Dissenters on all sides of you, and you will see at once that their Ministers, depending simply upon the people, become the *creatures* of the people. Are you content that this should be your case ? Alas ! can a greater evil befall Christians, than for their teachers to be guided by them, instead of guiding ? How can we " hold fast the form of sound words," and " keep that which is committed to our trust," if our influence is to depend simply on our popularity ? Is it not our very office to *oppose* the world ? can we then allow ourselves to *court* it ? to preach smooth .hings and prophesy deceits ? to make the way of life easy to the rich and indolent, and to bribe the humbler classes by excitements and strong intoxicating doctrine ? Surely it must not be so ;—and the question recurs, on *what* are we to rest our authority, when the State deserts us ?

CHRIST has not left His Church without claim of its own upon the attention of men. Surely not. Hard Master He cannot be, to bid us oppose the world, yet give us no credentials for so doing. There are some who rest their divine mission on their own unsupported assertion ; others, who rest it upon their popularity ; others, on their success ; and others, who rest it upon their temporal distinctions. This last case has, perhaps, been too much our own ; I fear we have neglected the real ground on which our authority is built,—OUR APOSTOLICAL DESCENT.

★ ★ ★

Therefore, my dear Brethren, act up to your professions. Let it not be said that you have neglected a gift ; for if you have the Spirit of the Apostles on you, surely this *is* a great gift. " Stir up the gift of God which is in you." Make much of it. Show your value of it. Keep it before your minds as an honorable badge, far higher than that secular respectability, or cultivation, or polish, or learning, or rank, which gives you a hearing with the many. Tell *them* of your gift. The times will soon drive you to do this, if you mean to be still any thing. But wait not for the times. Do not be compelled, by the world's forsaking you, to recur as if unwillingly to the high source of your authority. Speak out now, before you are forced, both as glorying in your privilege, and to ensure your rightful honor from your people. A notion has gone abroad, that they can take away your power. They think they have given and can take it away. They think it lies in the Church property, and they know that they have politically the power to confiscate that property. They have been deluded into a notion that present palpable usefulness, produceable results, acceptableness to your flocks, that these and such like are the tests of your Divine commission. Enlighten them in this matter. Exalt our Holy Fathers, the Bishops, as the Representatives of the Apostles, and the Angels of the Churches ; and magnify your office, as being ordained by them to take part in their Ministry.

But, if you will not adopt my view of the subject, which I offer to you, not doubtingly, yet (I hope) respectfully, at all events, CHOOSE YOUR SIDE. To remain neuter much longer will be itself to take a part. *Choose* your side ; since side you shortly must, with one or other party, even though you do nothing. Fear to be of those, whose line is decided for them by chance circumstances, and who may perchance find themselves with the enemies of CHRIST, while they think but to remove themselves from worldly politics. Such abstinence is impossible in troublous times. HE THAT IS NOT WITH ME, IS AGAINST ME, AND HE THAT GATHERETH NOT WITH ME SCATTERETH ABROAD.

Tract I

* * *

C

LIBERALISM

Ye cannot halve the Gospel of God's grace ;
  Men of presumptuous heart ! I know you well.
  Ye are of those who plan that we should dwell,
Each in his tranquil home and holy place ;
Seeing the Word refines all natures rude,
And tames the stirrings of the multitude.

And ye have caught some echoes of its lore,
  As heralded amid the joyous choirs ;
  Ye mark'd it spoke of peace, chastised desires,
Good-will and mercy,—and ye heard no more ;
But, as for zeal and quick-eyed sanctity,
And the dread depths of grace, ye pass'd them by.

And so ye halve the Truth ; for ye in heart.
  At best, are doubters whether it be true,
  The theme discarding, as unmeet for you,
Statesmen or Sages. O new-compass'd art
Of the ancient Foe !—but what, if it extends
O'er our own camp, and rules amid our friends ?

Verses on Various Occasions

I conclude this notice of Liberalism in Oxford, and the party which was antagonistic to it, with some propositions in detail, which, as a member of the latter, and together with the High Church, I earnestly denounced and abjured.

1. No religious tenet is important, unless reason shows it to be so.

Therefore, *e.g.* the doctrine of the Athanasian Creed is not to be insisted on, unless it tends to convert the soul ; and the doctrine of the Atonement is to be insisted on, if it does convert the soul.

2. No one can believe what he does not understand.

Therefore, *e.g.* there are no mysteries in true religion.

3. No theological doctrine is any thing more than an opinion which happens to be held by bodies of men.

Therefore, *e.g.* no creed, as such, is necessary for salvation.

4. It is dishonest in a man to make an act of faith in what he has not had brought home to him by actual proof.

Therefore, *e.g.* the mass of men ought not absolutely to believe in the divine authority of the Bible.

5. It is immoral in a man to believe more than he can spontaneously receive as being congenial to his moral and mental nature.

Therefore, *e.g.* a given individual is not bound to believe in eternal punishment.

6. No revealed doctrines or precepts may reasonably stand in the way of scientific conclusions.

Therefore, *e.g.* Political Economy may reverse our Lord's declarations about poverty and riches, or a system of Ethics may teach that the highest condition of body is ordinarily essential to the highest state of mind.

7. Christianity is necessarily modified by the growth of civilization, and the exigencies of times.

Therefore, *e.g.* the Catholic priesthood, though necessary in the Middle Ages, may be superseded now.

8. There is a system of religion more simply true than Christianity as it has ever been received.

Therefore, *e.g.* we may advance that Christianity is the " corn of wheat " which has been dead for 1800 years, but at length will bear fruit ; and that Mahometanism is the manly religion, and existing Christianity the womanish.

9. There is a right of Private Judgment : that is, there is no existing authority on earth competent to interfere with the liberty of individuals in reasoning and judging for themselves about the Bible and its contents, as they severally please.

Therefore, *e.g.* religious establishments requiring subscription are Anti-christian.

10. There are rights of conscience such, that every one may lawfully advance a claim to profess and teach what is false and wrong in matters, religious, social, and moral, provided that to his private conscience it seems absolutely true and right.

Therefore, *e.g.* individuals have a right to preach and practise fornication and polygamy.

11. There is no such thing as a national or state conscience.

Therefore, *e.g.* no judgments can fall upon a sinful or infidel nation.

12. The civil power has no positive duty, in a normal state of things, to maintain religious truth.

Therefore, *e.g.* blasphemy and sabbath-breaking are not rightly punishable by law.

13. Utility and expedience are the measure of political duty.

Therefore, *e.g.* no punishment may be enacted, on the ground that God commands it : *e.g.* on the text, " Whoso sheddeth man's blood, by man shall his blood be shed."

14. The Civil Power may dispose of Church property without sacrilege.

Therefore, *e.g.* Henry VIII. committed no sin in his spoliations.

15. The Civil Power has the right of ecclesiastical jurisdiction and administration.

Therefore, *e.g.* Parliament may impose articles of faith on the Church or suppress Dioceses.

16. It is lawful to rise in arms against legitimate princes.

Therefore, *e.g.* the Puritans in the 17th century, and the French in the 18th, were justifiable in their Rebellion and Revolution respectively.

17. The people are the legitimate source of power.

Therefore, *e.g.* Universal Suffrage is among the natural rights of man.

18. Virtue is the child of knowledge, and vice of ignorance.

Therefore, *e.g.* education, periodical literature, railroad travelling, ventilation, drainage, and the arts of life, when fully carried out, serve to make a population moral and happy.

All of these propositions, and many others too, were familiar to me thirty years ago, as in the number of the tenets of Liberalism, and, while I gave into none of them except No. 12, and perhaps No. 11, and partly No. 1, before I began to publish, so afterwards I wrote against most of them in some part or other of my Anglican works

Apologia

THE WORLD

The world overcomes us, not merely by appealing to our reason, or by exciting our passions, but by imposing on our imagination. So much do the systems of men swerve from the Truth as set forth in Scripture, that their very presence becomes a standing fact against Scripture, even when our reason condemns them, by their persevering assertions, and they gradually overcome those who set out by contradicting them. In all cases, what is often and unhesitatingly asserted, at length finds credit with the mass of mankind ; and so it happens, in this instance, that, admitting as we do from the first, that the world is one of our three chief enemies, maintaining, rather than merely granting, that the outward face of things speaks a different language from the word of God ; yet, when we come to act in the world, we find this very thing a trial, not merely of our obedience, but even of our faith ; that is, the mere fact that the world turns out to be what we began by actually confessing concerning it.

★　★　★

The world really brings no new argument to its aid,—nothing beyond its own assertion. In the very outset Christians allow that its teaching is contrary to Revelation, and not to be taken as authority ; nevertheless, afterwards, this mere unargumentative teaching, which, when viewed in theory, formed no objection to the truth of the Inspired Word, yet, when actually heard in the intercourse of life, converts them, more or less, to the service of the " prince of the power of the air, the spirit which now worketh in the children of disobedience." It assails their *imagination*. The world sweeps by in long procession ;—its principalities and powers, its Babel of languages, the astrologers of Chaldæa, the horse and its rider and the chariots of Egypt, Baal and Ashtoreth and their false worship ; and those who witness, feel its fascination ; they flock after it ; with a strange fancy, they ape its gestures, and dote upon its mummeries; and then, should they perchance fall in with the simple solemn services of Christ's Church, and hear her witnesses going the round of Gospel truths as when they left them: "I am the Way, the Truth, and the Life;" "Be sober, be vigilant;" "Strait is the gate, narrow the way;" "If any man will come after Me, let him deny himself;" "He is despised and rejected of men, a Man of sorrows and acquainted with grief:"—how utterly unreal do these appear, and the preachers of them, how irrational, how puerile !—how extravagant in their opinions, how weak in their reasoning !— and if they profess to pity and bear with them, how nearly does their compassion border on contempt !

★   ★   ★

Meanwhile, it is an encouragement to us to think how much may be done in way of protest and teaching, by the mere example of those who endeavour to serve God faithfully. In this way we may use against the world its own weapons; and, as its success lies in the mere boldness of assertion with which it maintains that evil is good, so by the counter-assertions of a strict life and a resolute profession of the truth, we may retort upon the imaginations of men, that religious obedience is not impracticable, and that Scripture has its persuasives. A martyr or a confessor is a fact, and has its witness in itself; and, while it disarranges the theories of human wisdom, it also breaks in upon that security and seclusion into which men of the world would fain retire from the thought of religion. . . . Confessors have a witness even in the breasts of those who oppose them, an instinct originally from God, which may indeed be perverted into a hatred, but scarcely into an utter disregard of the Truth, when exhibited before them. The instance cannot be found in the history of mankind, in which an anti-Christian power could long abstain from persecuting. The disdainful Festus at length impatiently interrupted his prisoner's speech; and in our better-regulated times, whatever be the scorn or malevolence which is directed against the faithful Christian, these very feelings show that he is really a restraint on vice and unbelief, and a warning and guide to the feeble-minded, and to those who still linger in the world with hearts more religious than their professed opinions ; and thus even literally, . . . he overcomes the world, conquering while he suffers, and willingly accepting overbearing usage and insult from others, so that he may in some degree benefit them, though the more abundantly he loves them, the less he be loved.

Oxford University Sermons

THE CHURCH IN HISTORY

But in truth the whole course of Christianity from the first, when we come to examine it, is but one series of troubles and disorders. Every century is like every other, and to those who live in it seems worse than all times before it. The Church is ever ailing, and lingers on in weakness, "always bearing about in the body the dying of the Lord Jesus, that the life also of Jesus might be made manifest in her body." Religion seems ever expiring, schisms dominant, the light of Truth dim, its adherents scattered. The cause of Christ is ever in its last agony, as though it were but a question of time whether it fails finally this day or another. The Saints are ever all but failing from the earth, and Christ all but coming ; and thus the Day of Judgment is literally ever at hand ; and it is our duty ever to be looking out for it, not disappointed that we have so often said, "now is the moment," and that at the last, contrary to our expectation, Truth has somewhat rallied. Such is God's will, gathering in His elect, first one and then another, by little and little, in the intervals of sunshine between storm and storm, or snatching them from the surge of evil, even when the waters rage most furiously. Well may prophets cry out, "How long will it be, O Lord, to the end of these wonders ? " how long will this perishing world be sustained by the feeble lights which struggle for existence in its unhealthy atmosphere ? God alone knows the day and the hour when that will at length be, which He is ever threatening ; meanwhile, thus much of comfort do we gain from what has been hitherto,—not to despond, not to be dismayed, not to be anxious, at the troubles which encompass us. They have ever been ; they ever shall be ; they are our portion. "The floods are risen, the floods have lift up their voice, the floods lift up their waves. The waves of the sea are mighty, and rage horribly ; but yet the Lord, who dwelleth on high, is mightier."

Via Media

This, then, is one trial of Faith. Another, which has in all ages assailed it, and not the least in our own age, is the success which attends measures or institutions which are not in accordance with the revealed rule of duty. This was the perplexity of believers in the old time, as we read in the Psalms and Prophets, viz. that the wicked should prosper, while God's servants seemed to fail : and so in Gospel times. Not that the Church has not this peculiar prerogative with it, which no other religious body has, that as it began with Christ's first coming, so it will never fail till He comes again ; but that for a time, in the course of single generations, nay, I may say in every age and at all times, it seems to be failing, and its enemies to be prevailing. It is the peculiarity of the warfare between the Church and the world, that the world seems ever gaining on the Church, yet the Church is really ever gaining on the world. Its enemies are ever triumphing over it as vanquished, and its members ever despairing ; yet it abides. It abides, and it sees the ruin of its oppressors and enemies. " O how suddenly do they consume, perish, and come to a fearful end ! " Kingdoms rise and fall ; nations expand and contract ; dynasties begin and end ; princes are born and die ; confederacies are made and unmade, and parties, and companies, and crafts, and guilds, and establishments, and philosophies, and sects, and heresies. They have their day, but the Church is eternal ; yet *in* their day they seem of much account. How in early times must the Church have been dismayed, when, from the East, the false religion of Mahomet spread far and near, and Christians were extirpated or converted by it by thousands ! Yet even that long-lived delusion is now failing ; and though younger than the Church by some centuries, has aged before it. And so in like manner, in spite of the duration of the Christian name hitherto, much there is to try our faith at this moment, who cannot see the future, and therefore cannot see the short duration of what shows proudly and successfully now. We at this day see a number of philosophies, sects, and parties, thriving and extending, and the Church seems poor and helpless, as if its very place were to be insulted, and its very calling to give way. We see men in one department of philosophy rejecting the accounts, for instance, of the Creation or the Deluge, as they stand in the Old Testament ; others setting aside the precepts of almsgiving, and the like, as given in the New ; others disputing the historical narratives contained in the Old ; and others denying those interpretations of the doctrinal portion of Scripture which have ever been received. We see imperfect forms of Christianity made the religion of states and nations, and apparently bringing forth good fruit ; nay, apparently flourishing more than many forms which are more perfect and catholic. We see the Church in slavery apparently flourishing more than the Church free. We see sects apparently flourishing more than the Church. We see wrong principles, unsound doctrines, apparently making men what Christians should be, and what the true Gospel can alone really make any one. We find the teachers of what we must call heresy, and the ministers of division, doing what the Church does not, or cannot do ; we find dissenting bodies sending missions to the heathen, and apparently succeeding in converting them. I do not speak of the fact, that good men are found among bodies which are not in communion with the Church. This is no difficulty to faith. That God who raised up Elijah and Elisha in Israel, has no where said He will not now also extend His mercies wider than His promises : but I speak of the apparent infringement of His promises in the visible disorders of the Church, and the triumph of other bodies over it. When we dwell on such facts as these, I do think it requires some special faith in those who are exposed to the temptation, to keep close to the ancient ways of the Church Catholic, and to remain untouched by the sophistries and unmoved by the successes, of this world which surrounds us.

Sermons on Subjects of the Days

THE RELIGION OF THE WORLD

In every age of Christianity, since it was first preached, there has been what may be called a *religion of the world,* which so far imitates the one true religion, as to deceive the unstable and unwary. The world does not oppose religion *as such.* I may say, it never has opposed it. In particular, it has, in all ages, acknowledged in one sense or other the Gospel of Christ, fastened on one or other of its characteristics, and professed to embody this in its practice ; while by neglecting the other parts of the holy doctrine, it has, in fact, distorted and corrupted even that portion of it which it has exclusively put forward, and so has contrived to explain away the whole ;—for he who cultivates only one precept of the Gospel to the exclusion of the rest, in reality attends to no part at all. Our duties *balance* each other ; and though we are too sinful to perform them all perfectly, yet we may in some measure be performing them all, and preserving the balance on the whole ; whereas to give ourselves only to this or that commandment, is to incline our minds in a wrong direction, and at length to pull them down to the earth. . . .

* * *

What is the world's religion now ? It has taken the brighter side of the Gospel,—its tidings of comfort, its precepts of love ; all darker, deeper views of man's condition and prospects being comparatively forgotten. This is the religion *natural* to a civilized age, and well has Satan dressed and completed it into an idol of the Truth. As the reason is cultivated, the taste formed, the affections and sentiments refined, a general decency and grace will of course spread over the face of society, quite independently of the influence of Revelation. That beauty and delicacy of thought, which is so attractive in books, then extends to the conduct of life, to all we have, all we do, all we are. Our manners are courteous ; we avoid giving pain or offence ; our words become correct ; our relative duties are carefully performed. Our sense of propriety shows itself even in our domestic arrangements, in the embellishments of our houses, in our amusements, and so also in our religious profession. Vice now becomes unseemly and hideous to the imagination, or, as it is sometimes familiarly said, " out of taste." Thus elegance is gradually made the test and standard of virtue, which is no longer thought to possess an intrinsic claim on our hearts, or to exist, *further than* it leads to the quiet and comfort of others. Conscience is no longer recognized as an independent arbiter of actions, its authority is explained away ; partly it is superseded in the minds of men by the so-called moral sense, which is regarded merely as the love of the beautiful ; partly by the rule of expediency, which is forthwith substituted for it in the details of conduct. Now conscience is a stern, gloomy principle ; it tells us of guilt and of prospective punishment. Accordingly, when its terrors disappear, then disappear also, in the creed of the day, those fearful images of Divine wrath with which the Scriptures abound. They are explained away. Every thing is bright and cheerful. Religion is pleasant and easy ; benevolence is the chief virtue ; intolerance, bigotry, excess of zeal, are the first of sins. Austerity is an absurdity ;—even firmness is looked on with an unfriendly, suspicious eye. On the other hand, all open profligacy is discountenanced ; drunkenness is accounted a disgrace ; cursing and swearing are vulgarities. Moreover, to a cultivated mind, which recreates itself in the varieties of literature and knowledge, and is interested in the ever-accumulating discoveries of science, and the ever-fresh accessions of information, political or otherwise, from foreign countries, religion will commonly seem to be dull, from want of novelty. Hence excitements are eagerly sought out and rewarded. New objects in religion, new systems and plans, new doctrines, new preachers, are necessary to satisfy that craving which the so-called spread of knowledge has created. The mind becomes morbidly sensitive and fastidious ; dissatisfied with things as they are, desirous of a change *as such,* as if alteration must of itself be a relief.

Now I would have you . . . consider whether such a state of refinement as I have attempted to describe, is not that to which men might be brought, quite independent of religion, by the mere influence of education and civilization ; and then again, whether, nevertheless, this mere refinement of mind is not more or less all that is called religion at this day. . . . I do not at all deny that this spirit of the world uses words, and makes professions, which it would not adopt except for the suggestions of Scripture ; nor do I deny that it takes a general colouring from Christianity, so as really to be modified by it, nay, in a measure enlightened and exalted by it. Again, I fully grant that many persons in whom this bad spirit shows itself, are but partially infected by it, and at bottom, good Christians, though imperfect. Still, after all, here is an existing teaching, only partially evangelical, built upon worldly principle, yet pretending to be the Gospel, dropping one whole side of the Gospel, its austere character, and considering it enough to be benevolent, courteous, candid, correct in conduct, delicate,— though it includes no true fear of God, no fervent zeal for His honour, no deep hatred of sin, no horror at the sight of sinners, no indignation and compassion at the blasphemies of heretics, no jealous adherence to doctrinal truth, no especial sensitiveness about the particular means of gaining ends, provided the ends be good, no loyalty to the Holy Apostolic Church, of which the Creed speaks, no sense of the authority of religion as external to the mind : in a word, no seriousness,—and therefore is neither hot nor cold, but (in scripture language) *lukewarm*. Thus the present age is the very contrary to what are commonly called the dark ages ; and together with the faults of those ages we have lost their virtues. I say their virtues ; for even the errors then prevalent, a persecuting spirit, for instance, fear of religious inquiry, bigotry, these were, after all, but perversions and excesses of *real virtues,* such as zeal and reverence ; and we, instead of limiting and purifying them, have taken them away root and branch. Why ? because we have not acted from a love of the Truth, but from the influence of the Age. The old generation has passed, and its character with it ; a new order of things has arisen. Human society has a new frame-work, and fosters and developes a new character of mind ; and this new character is made by the enemy of our souls, to resemble the Christian's obedience as near as it may, its likeness all the time being but accidental. . . .

* * *

The form of doctrine, which I have called the religion of the day, is especially adapted to please men of sceptical minds, . . . who have never been careful to obey their conscience, who cultivate the intellect without disciplining the heart, and who allow themselves to speculate freely about what religion *ought to be,* without going to Scripture to discover what it really is. Some persons of this character almost consider religion itself to be an obstacle in the advance of our social and political well-being. But they know human nature requires it ; therefore they select the most *rational* form of religion (so they call it) which they can find. Others are far more seriously disposed, but are corrupted by bad example or other cause. But they *all* discard (what they call) gloomy views of religion ; they all trust themselves more than God's word, and thus may be classed together ; and are ready to embrace the pleasant consoling religion natural to a polished age. They lay much stress on works on *Natural Theology,* and think that all religion is contained in these ; whereas, in truth, there is no greater fallacy than to suppose such works to be in themselves in any true sense religious at all. Religion, it has been well observed, is something *relative to us* ; a system of commands and promises from God *towards* us. But how are we concerned with the sun, moon, and stars ? or with the laws of the universe ? how will they teach us our *duty* ? how will they speak to *sinners* ? They do not speak to sinners at all. They were created *before* Adam fell. They " declare the *glory* of God," but not His *will.* They are all perfect, all harmonious ; but that brightness and excellence which they exhibit in their own creation, and the Divine benevolence therein seen, are of little moment to fallen man. We see nothing there of God's *wrath,* of which the conscience of a sinner loudly speaks. So that there cannot be a more dangerous (though a common) device of Satan, than to carry us off from our own secret thoughts, to make us forget our own hearts, which tell us of a God of justice and holiness, and to fix our attention merely on the God who made the heavens ; who is *our* God indeed, but not God as manifested to us sinners, but as He shines forth to His Angels, and to His elect hereafter.

* * *

This indeed is the creed of shallow men, in *every* age, who reason a little, and feel not at all, and who think themselves enlightened and philosophical. Part of what they say is false, part is true, but misapplied ; but why I have noticed it here, is to show how exactly it fits in with what I have already described as the peculiar religion of a civilized age ; it fits in with it equally well as does that of the (so-called) religious world, which is the opposite extreme.

* * *

Here I will not shrink from uttering my firm conviction, that it would be a gain to this country, were it vastly more superstitious, more bigoted, more gloomy, more fierce in its religion, than at present it shows itself to be. Not, of course, that I think the tempers of mind herein implied desirable, which would be an evident absurdity ; but I think them infinitely more desirable and more promising than a heathen obduracy, and a cold, self-sufficient, self-wise tranquillity.

Parochial and Plain Sermons

DOGMATIC RELIGION

A

Is not the being of a God reported to us by testimony, handed down by history, inferred by an inductive process, brought home to us by metaphysical necessity, urged on us by the suggestions of our conscience ? It is a truth in the natural order, as well as in the supernatural. So much for its origin ; and, when obtained, what is it worth ? Is it a great truth or a small one ? Is it a comprehensive truth ? Say that no other religious idea whatever were given but it, and you have enough to fill the mind ; you have at once a whole dogmatic system. The word " God " is a Theology in itself, indivisibly one, inexhaustibly various, from the vastness and the simplicity of its meaning. Admit a God, and you introduce among the subjects of your knowledge, a fact encompassing, closing in upon, absorbing, every other fact conceivable. How can we investigate any part of any order of Knowledge, and stop short of that which enters into every order ? All true principles run over with it, all phenomena converge to it ; it is truly the First and the Last. In word indeed, and in idea, it is easy enough to divide Knowledge into human and divine, secular and religious, and to lay down that we will address ourselves to the one without interfering with the other ; but it is impossible in fact. Granting that divine truth differs in kind from human, so do human truths differ in kind one from another. If the knowledge of the Creator is in a different order from knowledge of the creature, so, in like manner, metaphysical science is in a different order from physical, physics from history, history from ethics. You will soon break up into fragments the whole circle of secular knowledge, if you begin the mutilation with divine.

I have been speaking simply of Natural Theology ; my argument of course is stronger when I go on to Revelation. Let the doctrine of the Incarnation be true : is it not at once of the nature of an historical fact, and of a metaphysical ? Let it be true that there are Angels : how is not this a point of knowledge in the same sense as the naturalist's asseveration, that myriads of living things might co-exist on the point of a needle? That the Earth is to be burned by fire, is, if true, as large a fact as that huge monsters once played amid its depths; that Antichrist is to come, is as categorical a heading to a chapter of history, as that Nero or Julian was Emperor of Rome; that a divine influence moves the will, is a subject of thought not more mysterious than the result of volition on our muscles, which we admit as a fact in metaphysics.

I do not see how it is possible for a philosophical mind, first, to believe these religious facts to be true; next, to consent to ignore them; and thirdly, in spite of this, to go on to profess to be teaching all the while *de omni scibili*. No; if a man thinks in his heart that these religious facts are short of truth, that they are not true in the sense in which the general fact and the law of the fall of a stone to the earth is true, I understand his excluding Religion from his University, though he professes other reasons for its exclusion. In that case the varieties of religious opinion under which he shelters his conduct, are not only his apology for publicly disowning Religion, but a cause of his privately disbelieving it. He does not think that any thing is known or can be known for certain, about the origin of the world or the end of man.

This, I fear, is the conclusion to which intellects, clear, logical, and consistent, have come, or are coming, from the nature of the case; and, alas! in addition to this *primâ-facie* suspicion, there are actual tendencies in the same direction in Protestantism, viewed whether in its original idea, or again in the so-called Evangelical movement in these islands during the last century. The religious world, as it is styled, holds, generally speaking, that Religion consists, not in knowledge, but in feeling or sentiment. The old Catholic notion, which still lingers in the Established Church, was, that Faith was an intellectual act, its object truth, and its result knowledge. Thus if you look into the Anglican Prayer Book, you will find definite *credenda*, as well as definite *agenda*; but in proportion as the Lutheran leaven spread, it became fashionable to say that Faith was, not an acceptance of revealed doctrine, not an act of the intellect, but a feeling, an emotion, an affection, an appetency; and, as this view of Faith obtained, so was the connexion of Faith with Truth and Knowledge more and more either forgotten or denied. . . . There was, it appeared, a demand for Religion, and therefore there was a supply ; human nature could not do without Religion, any more than it could do without bread ; a supply was absolutely necessary, good or bad, and, as in the case of the articles of daily sustenance, an article which was really inferior was better than none at all. Thus Religion was useful, venerable, beautiful, the sanction of order, the stay of government, the curb of self-will and self-indulgence, which the laws cannot reach : but, after all, on what was it based ? Why, that was a question delicate to ask, and imprudent to answer ; but, if the truth must be spoken, however reluctantly, the long and the short of the matter was this, that Religion was based on custom, on prejudice, on law, on education, on habit, on loyalty, on feudalism, on enlightened expedience, on many, many things, but not at all on reason ; reason was neither its warrant, nor its instrument, and science had as little connexion with it as with the fashions of the season, or the state of the weather.

You see, Gentlemen, how a theory or philosophy, which began with the religious changes of the sixteenth century, has led to conclusions, which the authors of those changes would be the first to denounce, and has been taken up by that large and influential body which goes by the name of Liberal or Latitudinarian. . . .

*   *   *

At the risk of anticipating what I shall have occasion to insist upon in my next Discourse, let me say that, according to the teaching of Monotheism, God is an Individual, Self-dependent, All-perfect, Unchangeable Being ; intelligent, living, personal, and present ; almighty, all-seeing, all-remembering ; between whom and His creatures there is an infinite gulf ; who has no origin, who is all-sufficient for Himself ; who created and upholds the universe ; who will judge every one of us, sooner or later, according to that Law of right and wrong which He has written on our hearts. He is One who is sovereign over, operative amidst, independent of, the appointments which He has made ; One in whose hands are all things, who has a purpose in every event, and a standard for every deed, and thus has relations of His own towards the subject-matter of each particular science which the book of knowledge unfolds ; who has with an adorable, never-ceasing energy implicated Himself in all the history of creation, the constitution of nature, the course of the world, the origin of society, the fortunes of nations, the action of the human mind ; and who thereby necessarily becomes the subject-matter of a science, far wider and more noble than any of those which are included in the circle of Secular Education.

This is the doctrine which belief in a God implies in the mind of a Catholic : if it means any thing, it means all this, and cannot keep from meaning all this, and a great deal more ; and, even though there were nothing in the religious tenets of the last three centuries to disparage dogmatic truth, still, even then, I should have difficulty in believing that a doctrine so mysterious, so peremptory, approved itself as a matter of course to educated men of this day, who gave their minds attentively to consider it. . . .

The Idea of a University

B

Now what is Theology ? . . . By Theology, I simply mean the Science of God, or the truths we know about God put into system ; just as we have a science of the stars, and call it astronomy, or of the crust of the earth, and call it geology.

For instance, I mean, for this is the main point, that, as in the human frame there is a living principle, acting upon it and through it by means of volition, so, behind the veil of the visible universe, there is an invisible, intelligent Being, acting on and through it, as and when He will. Further, I mean that this invisible Agent is in no sense a soul of the world, after the analogy of human nature, but, on the contrary, is absolutely distinct from the world, as being its Creator, Upholder, Governor, and Sovereign Lord. Here we are at once brought into the circle of doctrines which the idea of God embodies. I mean then by the Supreme Being, one who is simply self-dependent, and the only Being who is such ; moreover, that He is without beginning or Eternal, and the only Eternal ; that in consequence He has lived a whole eternity by Himself ; and hence that He is all-sufficient, sufficient for His own blessedness, and all-blessed, and ever-blessed. Further, I mean a Being, who, having these prerogatives, has the Supreme Good, or rather is the Supreme Good, or has all the attributes of Good in infinite intenseness ; all wisdom, all truth, all justice, all love, all holiness, all beautifulness ; who is omnipotent, omniscient, omnipresent ; ineffably one, absolutely perfect ; and such, that what we do not know and cannot even imagine of Him, is far more wonderful that what we do and can. I mean One who is sovereign over His own will and actions, though always according to the eternal Rule of right and wrong, which is Himself. I mean, moreover, that He created all things out of nothing, and preserves them every moment, and could destroy them as easily as He made them ; and that, in consequence, He is separated from them by an abyss, and is incommunicable in all His attributes. And further, He has stamped upon all things, in the hour of their creation, their respective natures, and has given them their work and mission and their length of days, greater or less, in their appointed place. I mean, too, that He is ever present with His works, one by one, and confronts every thing He has made by His particular and most loving Providence, and manifests Himself to each according to its needs : and has on rational beings imprinted the moral law, and given them power to obey it, imposing on them the duty of worship and service, searching and scanning them through and through with His omniscient eye, and putting before them a present trial and a judgment to come.

Such is what Theology teaches about God, a doctrine, as the very idea of its subject-matter presupposes, so mysterious as in its fulness to lie beyond any system, and in particular aspects to be simply external to nature, and to seem in parts even to be irreconcilable with itself, the imagination being unable to embrace what the reason determines. It teaches of a Being infinite, yet personal ; all-blessed, yet ever operative ; absolutely separate from the creature, yet in every part of the creation at every moment ; above all things, yet under every thing. It teaches of a Being who, though the highest, yet in the work of creation, conservation, government, retribution, makes Himself, as it were, the minister and servant of all ; who, though inhabiting eternity, allows Himself to take an interest, and to have a sympathy, in the matters of space and time. His are all beings, visible and invisible, the noblest and the vilest of them. His are the substance, and the operation, and the results of that system of physical nature into which we are born. His too are the powers and achievements of the intellectual essences, on which He has bestowed an independent action and the gift of origination. The laws of the universe, the principles of truth, the relation of one thing to another, their qualities and virtues, the order and harmony of the whole, all that exists, is from Him ; and, if evil is not from Him, as assuredly it is not, this is because evil has no substance of its own, but is only the defect, excess, perversion, or corruption of that which has substance. All we see, hear, and touch, the remote sidereal firmament, as well as our own sea and land, and the elements which compose them, and the ordinances they obey, are His. The primary atoms of matter, their properties, their mutual action, their disposition and collocation, electricity, magnetism, gravitation, light, and whatever other subtle principles or operations the wit of man is detecting or shall detect, are the work of His hands. From Him has been every movement which has convulsed and re-fashioned the surface of the earth. The most insignificant or unsightly insect is from Him, and good in its kind ; the ever-teeming, inexhaustible swarms of animalculae, the myriads of living motes invisible to the naked eye, the restless ever-spreading vegetation which creeps like a garment over the whole earth, the lofty cedar, the umbrageous banana, are His. His are the tribes and families of birds and beasts, their graceful forms, their wild gestures, and their passionate cries.

And so in the intellectual, moral, social, and political world. Man, with his motives and works, his languages, his propagation, his diffusion, is from Him. Agriculture, medicine, and the arts of life, are His gifts. Society, laws, government, He is their sanction. The pageant of earthly royalty has the semblance and the benediction of the Eternal King. Peace and civilization, commerce and adventure, wars when just, conquest when humane and necessary, have His co-operation, and His blessing upon them. The course of events, the revolution of empires, the rise and fall of states, the periods and eras, the progresses and the retrogressions of the world's history, not indeed the incidental sin, over-abundant as it is, but the great outlines and the results of human affairs, are from His disposition. The elements and types and seminal principles and constructive powers of the moral world, in ruins though it be, are to be referred to Him. He " enlighteneth every man that cometh into this world." His are the dictates of the moral sense, and the retributive reproaches of conscience. To Him must be ascribed the rich endowments of the intellect, the irradiation of genius, the imagination of the poet, the sagacity of the politician, the wisdom (as Scripture calls it), which now rears and decorates the Temple, now manifests itself in proverb or in parable. The old saws of nations, the majestic precepts of philosophy, the luminous maxims of laws, the oracles of individual wisdom, the traditionary rules of truth, justice, and religion, even though imbedded in the corruption, or alloyed with the pride, of the world, betoken His original agency, and His long-suffering presence. Even where there is habitual rebellion against Him, or profound far-spreading social depravity, still the under-current, or the heroic outburst, of natural virtue, as well as the yearnings of the heart after what it has not, and its presentiment of its true remedies, are to be ascribed to the Author of all good. Anticipations or reminiscences of His glory haunt the mind of the self-sufficient sage, and of the pagan devotee ; His writing is upon the wall, whether of the Indian fane, or of the porticoes of Greece. He introduces Himself, He all but concurs, according to His good pleasure, and in His selected season, in the issues of unbelief, superstition, and false worship, and He changes the character of acts by His overruling operation. He condescends, though He gives no sanction, to the altars and shrines of imposture, and He makes His own fiat the substitute for its sorceries. He speaks amid the incantations of

Balaam, raises Samuel's spirit in the witch's cavern, prophesies of the Messias by the tongue of the Sibyl, forces Python to recognize His ministers, and baptizes by the hand of the mis-believer. He is with the heathen dramatist in his denunciations of injustice and tyranny, and his auguries of divine vengeance upon crime. Even on the unseemly legends of a popular mythology He casts His shadow, and is dimly discerned in the ode or the epic, as in troubled water or in fantastic dreams. All that is good, all that is true, all that is beautiful, all that is beneficent, be it great or small, be it perfect or fragmentary, natural as well as supernatural, moral as well as material, comes from Him.

The Idea of a University

REASON AND FAITH

The Discourses upon the relation of Faith to Reason . . . are of the nature of an exploring expedition into an all but unknown country, and do not even venture on a definition of either Faith or Reason on starting. As they proceed, however, they become more precise, as well as more accurate, in their doctrine, which shall here be stated in a categorical form, and, as far as possible, in the words used in the course of them.

1. Before setting down a definition of Faith and of Reason, it will be right to consider what is the popular notion of Faith and Reason, in contrast with each other.

2. According to this popular sense, Faith is the judging on weak grounds in religious matters, and Reason on strong grounds. Faith involves easiness, and Reason slowness in accepting the claims of Religion ; by Faith is meant a feeling or sentiment, by Reason an exercise of common sense ; Faith is conversant with conjectures or presumptions, Reason with proofs.

3. But now, to speak more definitely, what ought we to understand by the faculty of Reason largely understood ?

" By Reason is properly understood any process or act of the mind, by which, from knowing one thing, it advances on to know another."

4. The process of the Reasoning Faculty is either explicit or implicit : that is, either with or without a direct recognition, on the part of the mind, of the starting-point and path of thought from and through which it comes to its conclusion.

5. The process of reasoning, whether implicit or explicit, is the act of one and the same faculty, to which also belongs the power of analyzing that process, and of thereby passing from implicit to explicit. Reasoning, thus retrospectively employed in analyzing itself, results in a specific science or art, called logic, which is a sort of rhetoric, bringing out to advantage the implicit acts on which it has proceeded.

6. Again : there are two methods of reasoning—*à priori*, and *à posteriori* ; from antecedent probabilities or verisimilitudes,

and from evidence, of which the method of verisimilitude more naturally belongs to implicit reasoning, and the method of evidence to explicit.

7. Again :—though the Reasoning Faculty is in its nature one and the same in all minds, it varies, without limit, in point of strength, as existing in the concrete, that is, in individuals, and that, according to the subject-matter to which it is applied. Thus, a man may reason well on matters of trade, taken as his subject, but be simply unable to bring out into shape his reasoning upon them, or to write a book about them, because he has not the talent of analyzing—that is, of reasoning upon his own reasonings, or finding his own middle terms.

8. This inequality of the faculty in one and the same individual, with respect to different subject-matters, arises from two causes :—from want of experience and familiarity in the details of a given subject-matter ; and from ignorance of the principles or axioms, often recondite, which belong to it.

9. Hence there are three senses of the word " Reason," over and above the large and true sense. Since what is not brought out into view cannot be acknowledged as existing, it comes to pass that exercises of reasoning not explicit are commonly ignored. Hence by Reason, relatively to Religion, is meant, first, expertness in logical argument.

10. And again, since Evidences are more easily analyzed than verisimilitudes, hence reasonings, that is, investigations, on the subject of Religion, are commonly considered to be nothing but *à posteriori* arguments ; and Reason relatively to Religion becomes a faculty of framing Evidences. This, again, is a popular sense of the word, as applied to the subject of Religion, and a second sense in which I have used it.

11. The word " Reason " is still more often used in these Discourses in a third sense, viz., for a certain popular abuse of the faculty ; viz., when it occupies itself upon Religion, without a due familiar acquaintance with its subject-matter, or without a use of the first principles proper to it. This so-called Reason is in Scripture designated " the wisdom of the world ; " that is, the reasoning of secular minds about Religion, or reasonings about Religion based upon secular maxims, which are intrinsically foreign to it ; parallel to the abuse of Reason

in other subject-matters, as when chemical truths are made the axioms and starting-points in medical science, or the doctrine of final causes is introduced into astronomical or geological inquiries.

12. Faith is properly an assent, and an assent without doubt, or a certitude.

13. Since, in accepting a conclusion, there is a virtual recognition of its premisses, an act of Faith may be said (improperly) to include in it the reasoning process which is its antecedent, and to be in a certain aspect an exercise of Reason ; and thus is co-ordinate, and in contrast, with the three (improper) senses of the word " Reason " above enumerated, viz., explicit, evidential, and secular Reason.

14. Faith, viewed in contrast with Reason in these three senses, is implicit in its acts, adopts the method of verisimilitude, and starts from religious first principles.

15. Faith is kept from abuse, e.g. from falling into superstition, by a right moral state of mind, or such dispositions and tempers as religiousness, love of holiness and truth, etc.

Oxford University Sermons

REASON

A

I begin with what is of prime importance in [my critic's] charges against me—the sense in which I use the word "Reason," against which Reason I have made so many and such strong protests. It is a misleading word, as having various meanings. It is sometimes used to signify the gift which distinguishes man from brute ; I have not so used it. In this sense it is mainly a popular word, not a scientific. When so taken it is not a faculty of the mind, rather it is the mind itself ; or it is a generalization ; or it stands for the seat of all the mental powers together. For myself, I have taken it to mean the faculty of Reasoning in a large sense, nor do I know what other English word can be used to express that faculty. Besides, "Reason" is of a family of words all expressive of Reasoning. I may add that it is the meaning which Dr. Johnson puts upon the word, and the meaning which he traces through its derivative senses, corroborating his account of it by passages from English authors. "Reason," he says, is "the power by which man deduces one proposition from another, or proceeds from premisses to consequences ; the rational faculty ; discursive power." . . .

This being the recognised sense of the word, it is quite as important for my present purpose to show it to be the sense in which I have myself used "Reason" in what I have written at various times. . . . For instance :

First, I discard the vague popular sense of it as the distinguishing gift of man in contrast with the brute creation. "Sometimes," I say, "it stands for all in which man differs from the brutes ; and so it includes in its signification the faculty of distinguishing between right and wrong and the directing principle of conduct. In this sense certainly I do not here use it." (*U.S.*, p. 58.)

This is but a negative account of it, but in another Sermon I speak more distinctly. "By the exercise of reason is properly meant any process or act of the mind, by which, from knowing one thing, it advances on to know another." (*Ibid.*, p. 223.)

Again : " It is obvious that even our senses convey us but a little way out of ourselves, and introduce us to the external world only under circumstances, under conditions of time and place, and of certain media through which they act. We must be near things to touch them ; we must be interrupted by no simultaneous sounds in order to hear them ; we must have light to see them ; we can neither see, hear, nor touch things past or future. Now, Reason is that faculty of the mind by which this deficiency is supplied ; by which knowledge of things external to us—of beings, facts, and events—is attained beyond the range of sense ; . . . it brings us knowledge, whether clear or uncertain, still knowledge, in whatever degree of perfection, from every side ; but, at the same time, with this characteristic, that it obtains it indirectly, not directly, . . . on the hypothesis of something else . . . being assumed to be true." (*Ibid.*, p. 206.)

And again : " Reason, according to the simplest view of it, is the faculty of gaining knowledge without direct perception, or of ascertaining one thing by means of another. In this way it is able, from small beginnings, to create to itself a world of ideas, which do or do not correspond to the things themselves for which they stand, or are true or not according as it is exercised soundly or otherwise." (*Ibid.*, p. 256.)

These passages of mine are on subjects of their own ; but they will serve the purpose of making clear the account which in times past, as now, I have given of the reasoning faculty ; and, in doing so, I have implied how great a faculty it is. In its versatility, its illimitable range, its subtlety, its power of concentrating many ideas on one point, it is for the acquisition of knowledge all-important or rather necessary, with this drawback, however, in its ordinary use, that in every exercise of it, it depends for success upon the assumption of prior acts similar to that which it has itself involved, and therefore is reliable only conditionally. Its process is a passing from an antecedent to a consequent, and according as the start so is the issue. In the province of religion, if it be under the happy guidance of the moral sense, and with teachings which are not only assumptions in form but certainties in fact, it will arrive at indisputable truth, and then the house is at peace ; but if it be in the hands of enemies, who are under the delusion that their arbitrary assumptions are self-evident axioms, the reasoning will start from false premisses, and the mind will be in a state of melancholy disorder. But in no case need the reasoning faculty itself be to blame or responsible, except when identified with the assumptions of which it is the instrument. . . .

Such, in accordance with received English literature, is the sense in which I have used the word "Reason," and not in the sense of foreign writers. It must by no means then be supposed that I think a natural faculty of man to have been revolutionized, because an enemy of truth has availed itself of it for evil purposes. This is what [my critic] imputes to me, for I hold, it seems, that "in spite of the conscience there is" not a little "latent atheism in the nature, and especially in the reason, of man." Here he has been misled by the epithets which I attached in the *Apologia* to the Reason, as viewed in its continuous strenuous action against religious truth, both in and outside the Catholic body. I will explain why I did so. I had been referring to the fall of man, and our Catechisms tell us that the Fall opened upon him three great spiritual enemies, the World, the Flesh, and the Devil, which need to be resisted by means natural and supernatural. I was led by my general subject to select one of the three for my remarks, and to ask how it acted, and by what instruments? The instruments of the Evil One are best known to himself; the Flesh needs no instruments; the Reasoning Faculty is the instrument of the World. The World is that vast community impregnated by religious error which mocks and rivals the Church by claiming to be its own witness, and to be infallible. Such is the World, the False Prophet (as I called it fifty years ago), and Reasoning is its voice. I had in my mind such Apostolic sayings as "Love not the world, neither the things of the world," and "A friend of the world is the enemy of God"; but I was very loth, as indeed I am also now on the present occasion, to *preach*. Instead then of saying "the World's Reason," I said "Reason actually and historically," "Reason in fact and concretely in fallen man," "Reason in the educated intellect of England, France, and Germany," Reason in "every Government and every civilization through the world which

is under the influence of the European mind," Reason in the
"wild living intellect of man," which needs (to have) "its
stiff neck bent," that ultra "freedom of thought, which is in
itself one of the greatest of our natural gifts," "that deep,
plausible scepticism" which is "the development of human
reason as practically exercised by the natural man." That is,
Reason as wielded by the Living World, against the teaching
of the Infallible Church. . . .

In thus shifting the blame of hostility to religion from man
reasoning to man collective, I may seem to be imputing to a
divine ordinance (for such human society is) what I have dis-
claimed to be imputing to man's gift of reason ; but this is
to mistake my meaning. The World is a collection of individual men, and any one of them may hold and take on himself
to profess unchristian doctrine, and do his best to propagate
it ; but few have the power for such a work, or the opportunity.
It is by their union into one body, by the intercourse of man
with man and the sympathy thence arising, that error spreads
and becomes an authority. Its separate units which make up
the body rely upon each other, and upon the whole, for the
truth of their assertions ; and thus assumptions and false
reasonings are received without question as certain truths, on
the credit of alternate appeals and mutual cheers and *imprimaturs*.

I should like, if I could, to give a specimen of these assumptions, and the reasonings founded on them, which in my
Apologia I considered to be "corrosive" of all religion ; but
before doing so, I must guard against misconstruction of what
I am proposing. First, I am not proposing to carry on an
argument . . . ; but I would gladly explain, or rather complete on particular points, the statements I have before now
made in several works about Faith and Reason. Next, I can
truly say that, neither in those former writings nor now, have
I particular authors in mind who are or are said to be prominent
teachers in what I should call the School of the World. Such
an undertaking would require a volume, instead of half a dozen
pages such as these, and the study too of many hard questions ;
and I repeat, here I am attempting little more than to fill up a
few of the *lacunae* to be found in a chapter of the *Apologia,*
which, like the rest of the book, had to be written *extempore* ;

certainly I have no intention here of entering into controversy. And further, I wish to call attention to a passage in one of my St. Mary's Sermons, headed, " The World our Enemy," which is not directly on the subject of religious error, but still is applicable when I would fain clear myself in what I am saying of falling unintentionally into any harsh and extreme judgments. A few sentences will be enough to show the drift with which I quote it.

" There is a question," I say, " which it will be well to consider, viz., how far the world is a separate body from the Church of God. The two are certainly contrasted in Scripture, but the Church, so far from being literally and in fact separate from the world, is within it. The Church is a body, gathered together indeed in the world, but only in a process of separation from it. The world's power is over the Church, because the Church has gone forth into the world to save the world. All Christians are in the world and of the world, so far as Evil still has dominion over them, and not even the best of us is clean every whit from sin. Though then, in our idea of the one and the other, and in their principles and in their future prospects, the Church is one thing and the World is another, yet in present matter of fact the Church is of the World, not separate from it ; for the grace of God has but partial possession even of religious men, and the best that can be said of us is that we have two sides, a light side and a dark, and that the dark happens to be the outermost. Thus we form part of the world to each other, though we be not *of* the world. Even supposing there were a society of men influenced individually by Christian motives, still, this society, viewed as a whole, would be a worldly one ; I mean a society holding and maintaining many errors, and countenancing many bad practices. Evil ever floats on the top " (*P.S.*, VII, p. 35-36). In accordance with these cautions I will here avow that good men may imbibe to their great disadvantage the spirit of the world, and, on the contrary, inferior men may keep themselves comparatively clear of it.

These explanations being made, I take up the serious protest which I began in the *Apologia*. I say then that if, as I believe, the world, which the Apostles speak of so severely as a False Prophet (*U.S.*, VII), is identical with what we call human

Society now, then there never was a time since Christianity was, when, together with the superabundant temporal advantages which by it may come to us, it had the opportunity of being a worse enemy to religion and religious truth than it is likely to be in the years now opening upon mankind. I say so, because in its width and breadth it is so much better educated and informed than it ever was before, and because of its extent, so multiform and almost ubiquitous. Its conquests in the field of physical science, and its intercommunion of place with place, are a source to it both of pride and of enthusiasm. It has triumphed over time and space ; knowledge it has proved to be emphatically power ; no problems of the universe—material, moral, or religious—are too great for its ambitious essay and its high will to master. There is one obstacle in its path, I mean the province of religion. But can religion hope to be successful ? It is thought to be already giving way before the presence of what the world considers a new era in the history of man.

With these thoughts in my mind, I understand how it has come to pass, what has struck me as remarkable, that the partizans and spokesmen of Society, when they come to the question of religion, seem to care so little about proving what they maintain, and, on the warrant of their philosophy, are content silently and serenely to take by implication their first principles for granted, as if, like the teachers of Christianity, they were inspired and infallible. To the World, indeed, its own principles are infallible, and need no proof. Now if its representatives would but be candid, and say that their assumptions, as ours, are infallible, we should know where they stand ; there would be an end of controversy. As I have said before now, " Half the controversies in the world, could they be brought to a plain issue, would be brought to a prompt termination. Parties engaged in them would then perceive . . . that in substance . . . their difference was of first principles. . . . When men understand what each other means, they see for the most part that controversy is either superfluous or hopeless " (U.S., pp. 200–201). The World, then, has its first principles of religion, and so have we. If this were understood, I should not have any present cause of protest against its Reason as corrosive of our faith. I do not grudge the World its gods, its principles, and its worship ; but I protest against its sending them into Christian lecture rooms, libraries, societies, and companies, as if they were Christian—criticising, modelling, measuring, altering, improving, as it thinks, our doctrines, principles, and methods of thought, which we refer to divine informants. One of my *University Sermons,* in 1831, is on this subject ; it is called " The Usurpations of Reason," and I have nothing to change in the substance of it. I was very jealous of " the British Association " at its commencement, not as if science were not a divine gift, but because its first members seemed to begin with a profession of Theism, when I said their business was to keep to their own range of subjects. I argued that if they began with Theism, they would end with Atheism. At the end of half a century I have still more reason to be suspicious of the upshot of secular schools. Not, of course, that I suppose that the flood of unbelief will pour over us in its fulness at once. A large inundation requires a sufficient time, and there are always in the worst times witnesses for the Truth to stay the plague. Above all things there is the Infallible Church, of which I spoke so much in the *Apologia.* . . .

Stray Essays on Controversial Points

★   ★   ★

B

If to deny the omnipotence of reason in the discovery of truth is scepticism, I am in good company.

Let me take a more exact and adequate definition of scepticism, and see if I fall under it. The definition of scepticism to which I am myself accustomed is such as this : " Scepticism is the system which holds that no certainty is attainable, as not in other things so not in questions of religious truth and error." How have I incurred this reproach ? On the contrary, I have not only asserted, with a strength of words which has sometimes incurred censure, my belief in religious truth, but have insisted on the certainty of such truth, and on Certitude as having a place among the constitutents of human thought ;—analysing it, discriminating it, and giving tests of it, with a direct apprehension and manipulation quite incompatible with my never asking myself whether intellectually I was in any sense a sceptic or not. It seems to me that the charge of scepticism which has been used against me elsewhere, as well as in England, is a mere idle word, serviceable in an intellectual combat ; and I think it would be more charitable in opponents if, instead of imputing it to any dissatisfaction which I have at any time expressed with certain arguments used in Catholic controversy, they ascribed it, not to an underlying scepticism as to the truths in dispute, but rather to an unmeasured and even reckless confidence in them, or, again, to an attempt to test the availableness at the present time of certain conventional proofs used for polemical purposes.

And now I come to . . . my account of Reason considered as the faculty of reasoning. . . .

Here, first, I must protest against its being magisterially ruled by [my critic] that the word Reason has one and one only definite scientific meaning, accepted by all authorities in metaphysics, and incapable of any other ; whereas, before coming to the question of particular words and phrases, I really wish it settled whether there is a recognised science of metaphysics at all. . . . I have no great remorse that for fifty years I have used my native tongue as a vehicle for religious and ethical discussions ; in this instance, indeed, with the sanction of a writer who is commonly called *par excellence* our lexicographer. Provided I am careful to record the senses in which I use words, it is not the part of a fair critic to take them in another sense, and in that sense to be tragic in his reprobation of them. My turn of mind has never led me towards metaphysics ; rather it has been logical, ethical, practical. As to the word " Reason," it would have been a strange digression had I, in speaking of the religious state of Europe, entered into an account of the faculties of the human mind and the analysis which has been made of them by various metaphysicians.

* * *

In this latitude and confusion of the terminology found among professed metaphysicians I think I have a right to my own way of regarding the faculty of Reason, whether I fail in it or not ; and that the more because, while I am following the English use of the word, it is a personal satisfaction to me to be able also to believe that I am adhering to the ecclesiastical. At least Gregory the 16th, Pius the 9th, and the Vatican Council, when they would speak of " proving " and of " demonstrating," refer the act of the mind to " human reason."

When, then, in times past I have wished to express my anxiety lest serious dangers might be in store for educated society, my first business was to determine what sense I ought to give to the word " Reason," claimed by Rationalists as if specially belonging to themselves. The only senses of it which I knew—nay, which I know of it now—are two : in one of the two senses it seems to be a synonyme for " Mind," as used in contrast with the condition of brutes. This is far too broad an account of it to be of service in such a purpose as my own, and in consequence I have been thrown of necessity on the sense which is its alternative, viz., that reason is the faculty of reasoning ; and though such a view of it does not suggest that venerable and sovereign idea which we usually attach to " Reason," still, as I was not writing metaphysics, but with an ethical and social view, I did not find any great inconvenience in taking the word in its popular, etymological, and, as I hope, ecclesiastical acceptation.

. . . But I have never thought . . . of leaving truth to so untrustworthy a protection as reasoning by itself would be to it. The mind without any doubt is made for truth. Still, it does not therefore follow that truth is its object in all its powers. The imagination is a wonderful faculty in the cause of truth, but it often subserves the purposes of error—so do our most innocent affections. Every faculty has its place. There is a faculty in the mind which acts as a complement to reasoning, and as having truth for its direct object thereby secures its use for rightful purposes. This faculty, viewed in its relation to religion, is, as I have before said, the moral sense ; but it has a wider subject-matter than religion, and a more comprehensive office and scope, as being " the apprehension of first principles," and Aristotle has taught me to call it $\nuοῦς$, or the *noetic* faculty.

How this faculty of $\nuοῦς$ bears upon the action of reasoning scarcely requires many words. I have considered Reasoning as an instrument—that is, an instrument for the use of other faculties, for who ever heard of an instrument without there being, as I have taken for granted, some distinct power to make use of it ? Now to know what the reasoning faculty needs for the purposes of religion we must consider it, not in its abstract idea, but in the concrete. When so viewed, it includes an antecedent and a consequent, and it is at once plain what is the connecting link between it and (for instance) the noetic faculty. The antecedent of the reasoning is that link ; for the matter (as it is called) of the antecedent belongs both to the reasoning and also to those other faculties, many or few, which have for their object the antecedent. Great faculty as reasoning certainly is, it is from its very nature in all subjects dependent upon other faculties. It receives from them the antecedent with which its action starts ; and when this antecedent is true, there is no longer in religious matters room for any accusation against it of scepticism. In such matters the independent faculty which is mainly necessary for its healthy working and the ultimate warrant of the reasoning act, I have hitherto spoken of as the moral sense ; but, as I have already said, it has a wider subject-matter than religion, and a larger name than moral sense, as including intuitions, and this is what Aristotle calls νοῦς.

Stray Essays on Controversial Points

In the text, then, a truth is expressed in the form of a proverb, which is implied all through Scripture as a basis on which its doctrine rests—viz. that there is no necessary connexion between the intellectual and moral principles of our nature ; that on religious subjects we may prove any thing or overthrow any thing, and can arrive at truth but accidentally, if we merely investigate by what is commonly called Reason, which is in such matters but the instrument at best, in the hands of the legitimate judge, spiritual discernment. When we consider how common it is in the world at large to consider the intellect as the characteristic part of our nature, the silence of Scripture in regard to it (not to mention its positive disparagement of it) is very striking. . . .

* * *

I propose now to make some remarks upon the place which Reason holds in relation to Religion, the light in which we should view it, and certain encroachments of which it is sometimes guilty ; and I think that, without a distinct definition of the word, which would carry us too far from our subject, I can make it plain what I take it to mean. Sometimes, indeed, it stands for all in which man differs from the brutes, and so includes in its signification the faculty of distinguishing between right and wrong, and the directing principle in conduct. In this sense I certainly do not here use it, but in that narrower signification, which it usually bears, as representing or synonymous with the intellectual powers, and as opposed as such to the moral qualities, and to Faith.

This opposition between Faith and Reason takes place in two ways, when either of the two encroaches upon the province of the other. It would be an absurdity to attempt to find out mathematical truths by the purity and acuteness of the moral sense. It is a form of this mistake which has led men to apply such Scripture communications as are intended for religious purposes to the determination of physical questions. This error is perfectly understood in these days by all thinking men. This was the usurpation of the schools of theology in former ages, to issue their decrees to the subjects of the Senses and the Intellect. No wonder Reason and Faith were at variance. The other cause of disagreement takes place when Reason is the aggressor, and encroaches on the province of Religion, attempting to judge of those truths which are subjected to another part of our nature, the moral sense. . . .

*   *   *

Why should we be desirous to disguise the fact, if it be such, that men distinguished, some for depth and originality of mind, others for acuteness, others for prudence and good sense in practical matters, yet have been indifferent to Revealed Religion,—why, unless we have some misconceived notion concerning the connexion between the intellect and the moral principle ? . . . The powers of the intellect (in that degree, at least, in which, in matter of fact, they are found amongst us) do not necessarily lead us in the direction of our moral instincts, or confirm them ; but if the agreement between the two be but matter of accident, what testimony do we gain from the mere Reason to the truths of Religion ?

Why should we be surprised that one faculty of our compound nature should not be able to do that which is the work of another ? It is as little strange that the mind, which has only exercised itself on matters of literature or science, and never submitted itself to the influence of divine perceptions, should be unequal to the contemplation of a moral revelation, as that it should not perform the office of the senses. . . .

*   *   *

From considerations such as the foregoing, it appears that exercises of Reason are either external, or at least only ministrative, to religious inquiry and knowledge : accidental to them, not of their essence ; useful in their place, but not necessary. But in order to obtain further illustrations, and a view of the importance of the doctrine which I would advocate, let us proceed to apply it to the circumstances of the present times. Here, first, in finding fault with the times, it is right to disclaim all intention of complaining of them. To murmur and rail at the state of things under which we find ourselves, and to prefer a former state, is not merely indecorous, it is absolutely unmeaning. We are ourselves necessary parts of the existing system, out of which we have individually grown into being, into our actual position in society. Depending, therefore, on the times as a condition of existence, in wishing for other times we are, in fact, wishing we had never been born. Moreover, it is ungrateful to a state of society, from which we daily enjoy so many benefits, to rail against it. Yet there is nothing unbecoming, unmeaning, or ungrateful in pointing out its faults and wishing them away.

In this day, then, we see a very extensive development of an usurpation which has been preparing, with more or less of open avowal, for some centuries,—the usurpation of Reason in morals and religion. In the first years of its growth it professed to respect the bounds of justice and sobriety : it was little in its own eyes ; but getting strength, it was lifted up ; and casting down all that is called God, or worshipped, it took its seat in the temple of God, as His representative. Such, at least, is the consummation at which the Oppressor is aiming ; which he will reach, unless He who rids His Church of tyrants in their hour of pride, look down from the pillar of the cloud, and trouble his host.

Now, in speaking of an usurpation of the Reason at the present day, stretching over the province of Religion, and in fact over the Christian Church, no admission is made concerning the degree of cultivation which the Reason has at present reached in the territory which it has unjustly entered. A tyrant need not be strong ; he keeps his ground by prescription and through fear. It is not the profound thinkers who intrude with their discussions and criticisms within the sacred limits of moral truth. A really philosophical mind, if unhappily it has ruined its own religious perceptions, will be silent ; it will understand that Religion does not lie in its way : it may disbelieve its truths, it may account belief in them a weakness, or, on the other hand, a happy dream, a delightful error, which it cannot itself enjoy ;—any how, it will not usurp. But men who know but a little, are for that very reason most under the power of the imagination, which fills up for them at pleasure those departments of knowledge to which they are strangers ; and, as the ignorance of abject minds shrinks from the spectres which it frames there, the ignorance of the self-confident is petulant and presuming.

The usurpations of the Reason may be dated from the Reformation. Then, together with the tyranny, the legitimate authority of the ecclesiastical power was more or less overthrown ; and in some places its ultimate basis also, the moral sense. One school of men resisted the Church ; another went farther, and rejected the supreme authority of the law of Conscience. Accordingly, Revealed Religion was in a great measure stripped of its proof ; for the existence of the Church had been its external evidence, and its internal had been supplied by the moral sense. Reason now undertook to repair the demolition it had made, and to render the proof of Christianity independent both of the Church and of the law of nature. From that time (if we take a general view of its operations) it has been engaged first in making difficulties by the mouth of unbelievers, and then claiming power in the Church as a reward for having, by the mouth of apologists, partially removed them.

Oxford University Sermons

THE INTRODUCTION OF RATIONALISTIC PRINCIPLES INTO REVEALED RELIGION

Rationalism is a certain abuse of Reason ; that is, a use of it for purposes for which it never was intended, and is unfitted. To rationalize in matters of Revelation is to make our reason the standard and measure of the doctrines revealed ; to stipulate that those doctrines should be such as to carry with them their own justification ; to reject them, if they come in collision with our existing opinions or habits of thought, or are with difficulty harmonized with our existing stock of knowledge. And thus a rationalistic spirit is the antagonist of Faith ; for Faith is, in its very nature, the acceptance of what our reason cannot reach, simply and absolutely upon testimony.

There is, of course, a multitude of cases in which we allowably and rightly accept statements as true, partly on reason, and partly on testimony. We supplement the information of others by our own knowledge, by our own judgment of probabilities ; and, if it be very strange or extravagant, we suspend our assent. This is undeniable ; still, after all, there are truths which are incapable of reaching us except on testimony, and there is testimony, which by and in itself, has an imperative claim on our acceptance.

As regards Revealed Truth, it is not Rationalism to set about to ascertain, by the exercise of reason, what things are attainable by reason, and what are not ; nor, in the absence of an express Revelation, to inquire into the truths of Religion, as they come to us by nature ; nor to determine what proofs are necessary for the acceptance of a Revelation, if it be given ; nor to reject a Revelation on the plea of insufficient proof ; nor, after recognizing it as divine, to investigate the meaning of its declarations, and to interpret its language ; nor to use its doctrines, as far as they can be fairly used, in inquiring into its divinity ; nor to compare and connect them with our previous knowledge, with a view of making them parts of a whole ; nor to bring them into dependence on each other, to trace their mutual relations, and to pursue them to their legitimate issues. This is not Rationalism ; but it is Rationalism to accept the Revelation, and then to explain it away ; to speak of it as the Word of God, and to treat it as the word of man ; to refuse to let it speak for itself ; to claim to be told the *why* and the *how* of God's dealings with us, as therein described, and to assign to Him a motive and a scope of our own ; to stumble at the partial knowledge which He may give us of them ; to put aside what is obscure, as if it had not been said at all ; to accept one half of what has been told us, and not the other half ; to assume that the contents of Revelation are also its proof ; to frame some gratuitous hypothesis about them, and then to garble, gloss and colour them, to trim, clip, pare away, and twist them, in order to bring them into conformity with the idea to which we have subjected them.

* * *

Conduct such as this, on so momentous a matter, is, generally speaking, traceable to one obvious cause. The Rationalist makes himself his own centre, not his Maker ; he does not go to God, but he implies that God must come to him. And this, it is to be feared, is the spirit in which multitudes of us act at the present day. Instead of looking out of ourselves, and trying to catch glimpses of God's workings, from any quarter,— throwing ourselves forward upon Him and waiting on Him, we sit at home bringing everything to ourselves, enthroning ourselves in our own views, and refusing to believe anything that does not force itself upon us as true. Our private judgment is made everything to us,—is contemplated, recognized, and consulted as the arbiter of all questions, and as independent of everything external to us. Nothing is considered to have an existence except so far forth as our minds discern it. The notion of half views and partial knowledge, of guesses, surmises, hopes and fears, of truths faintly apprehended and not under- stood, of isolated facts in the great scheme of Providence, in a word, the idea of Mystery, is discarded.

Hence a distinction is drawn between what is called Objective and Subjective Truth, and Religion is said to consist in a reception of the latter. By Objective Truth is meant the

Religious System considered as existing in itself, external to this or that particular mind : by Subjective, is meant that which each mind receives in particular, and considers to be such. To believe in Objective Truth is to throw ourselves forward upon that which we have but partially mastered or made subjective ; to embrace, maintain, and use general propositions which are larger than our own capacity, of which we cannot see the bottom, which we cannot follow out into their multiform details ; to come before and bow before the import of such propositions, as if we were contemplating what is real and independent of human judgment. Such a belief, implicit, and symbolized as it is in the use of creeds, seems to the Rationalist superstitious and unmeaning, and he consequently confines Faith to the province of Subjective Truth, or to the reception of doctrine, as, and so far as, it is met and apprehended by the mind, which will be differently, as he considers, in different persons, in the shape of orthodoxy in one, heterodoxy in another. That is, he professes to *believe* in that which he *opines* ; and he avoids the obvious extravagance of such an avowal by maintaining that the moral trial involved in Faith does not lie in the submission of the reason to external realities partially disclosed, but in what he calls that candid pursuit of truth which ensures the eventual adoption of that opinion on the subject, which is best for us individually, which is most natural according to the constitution of our own minds, and, therefore, divinely intended for us. I repeat, he owns that Faith, viewed with reference to its objects, is never more than an opinion, and is pleasing to God, not as an active principle apprehending definite doctrines, but as a result and fruit, and therefore an evidence of past diligence, independent inquiry, dispassionateness, and the like. Rationalism takes the words of Scripture as signs of Ideas ; Faith, of Things or Realities.

*   *   *

This is a fit place to make some remarks on the Scripture sense of the word Mystery. It may seem a contradiction in terms to call Revelation a Mystery ; but is not the book of the Revelation of St. John as great a mystery from beginning to end as the most abstruse doctrine the mind ever imagined ? yet it is even called a *Revelation*. How is this ? The answer is simple. No revelation can be complete and systematic, from the weakness of the human intellect ; *so far as* it is not such, it is mysterious. When nothing is revealed, nothing is known, and there is nothing to contemplate or marvel at ; but when something is revealed, and only something, for all cannot be, there are forthwith difficulties and perplexities. A Revelation is religious doctrine viewed on its illuminated side ; a Mystery is the selfsame doctrine viewed on the side unilluminated. Thus Religious Truth is neither light nor darkness, but both together ; it is like the dim view of a country seen in the twilight, with forms half extricated from the darkness, with broken lines, and isolated masses. Revelation, in this way of considering it, is not a revealed *system*, but consists of a number of detached and incomplete truths belonging to a vast system unrevealed, of doctrines and injunctions mysteriously connected together ; that is, connected by unknown media, and bearing upon unknown portions of the system. And in this sense we see the propriety of calling St. John's prophecies, though highly mysterious, yet a revelation.

Essays Critical and Historical I

THE RATIONALISTIC SPIRIT IN HISTORICAL INQUIRY

A

It is notorious that the English Church is destitute of an Ecclesiastical History ; Gibbon is almost our sole authority for subjects as near the heart of a Christian as any can well be. We do not indeed mean to say that Mr. Milman will supply this want ; rather we conceive him to hold that it is a want which ought not to be supplied. Our impression at least is,—we do not mean to state it as more than an impression,—that he considers Church histories, as such, to be nothing better than "tolerabiles ineptiae." His present volumes are rather the substitute than the supply of this desideratum in our ecclesiastical literature, and are meant to supersede the history of the Church by the history of Christianity. But we acknowledge even this as a boon ; without agreeing to Mr. Milman's historical views or doctrinal opinions, as what we shall presently say will show, we consider it to be impossible even for a Gibbon to write an uninstructive history of the Evangelical Dispensation ; and much less can Mr. Milman, who is not a Gibbon, but a clergy-man, fail to be useful to those who are in search of facts, and have better principles than his own to read them by. . . .

However, we shall be very unjust to Mr. Milman, unless we try carefully to place ourselves in the position which he has chosen for contemplating and delineating the Christian religion. Unless we succeed in this, we shall cruelly misunderstand him, as if he held certain opinions, when he does but state the premisses which practically involve them. It is obvious that the whole system of Revelation may be viewed in various, nay antagonist aspects. He who regards our Lord as man, does not in consequence deny that He is more than man ; and they who with Mr. Milman love to regard the whole Christian history as much as possible as a thing of earth, may be wise or unwise, reverent or irreverent, in so doing, may be attempting what is practicable or impracticable, may eventually be led on to commit themselves to positive errors about it, and may accordingly be wantonly trifling with serious matters, but cannot without unfairness be charged with an *ipso facto* denial of its heavenly character. The Christian history is " an outward visible sign of an inward spiritual grace : " whether the sign can be satisfactorily treated separate from the thing signified is another matter ; but it seems to be Mr. Milman's intention so to treat it, and he must be judged by that intention, not by any other which we choose to impute to him. Christianity has an external aspect and an internal ; it is human without, divine within. To attempt to touch the human element without handling also the divine, we may fairly deem unreal, extravagant, and sophistical ; we may feel the two to be one integral whole, differing merely in aspect, not in fact : we may consider that a writer has not mastered his own idea who resolves to take liberties with the body, and yet not insult the animating soul. So we do ; but all this is another matter ; such a person does not *mean* any harm ; nor does the writer who determines, as far as he can, to view the Christian as a secular fact, to the exclusion of all theological truth. He gives a representation of it, such as it would appear to a man of the world. This, at least, is our *primâ facie* view of Mr. Milman's book. . . .

* * *

Now let us see how much we are disposed to grant to Mr. Milman, and where we part company with him : in doing which we must be allowed to begin somewhat *ab ovo,* and for a while to exchange a critical for a didactic tone. We maintain then, as we have already said, that Christianity, nor Christianity only, but all God's dealings with His creatures, have two aspects, one external, one internal. What one of the earliest Fathers says of its highest ordinance, is true of it altogether, and of all other divine dispensations : they are twofold, " having one part heavenly, and one part earthly." This is the law of Providence here below ; it works beneath a veil, and what is visible in its course does but shadow out at most, and sometimes obscures and disguises what is invisible. The world in which we are placed has its own system of laws and principles, which, as far as our knowledge of it goes, is, when once set in motion, sufficient to account for itself,—as complete and independent as if there was nothing beyond it. Ordinarily speaking, nothing happens, nothing goes on in the world, but may be satisfactorily traced to some other event or fact in it, or has a sufficient result in other events or facts in it, without the necessity of our following it into a higher system of things in order to explain its existence, or to give it a meaning. We will not stop to dwell on exceptions to this general statement, or on the narrowness of our knowledge of things : but what is every day said and acted on proves that this is at least the impression made upon most minds by the course of things in which we find ourselves. The sun rises and sets on a law ; the tides ebb and flow upon a law ; the earth is covered with verdure or buried in the ocean, it grows old and it grows young again, by the operation of fixed laws. Life, whether vegetable or animal, is subjected to a similar external and general rule. Men grow to maturity, then decay, and die. Moreover, they form into society, and society has its principles. Nations move forward by laws which act as a kind of destiny over them, and which are as vigorous now as a thousand years ago. And these laws of the social and political world run into the physical, making all that is seen one and one only system ; a horse stumbles, and an oppressed people is rid of their tyrant ; a volcano changes populous cities into a dull lake ; a gorge has of old time opened, and the river rolls on, bearing on its bosom the destined site of some great mart, which else had never been. We cannot set limits either to the extent or to the minuteness of this wonderful web of causes and effects, in which all we see is involved. It reaches to the skies ; it penetrates into our very thoughts, habits, and will.

Such is confessedly the world in which our Almighty Creator has placed us. If then He is still actively present with His own work, present with nations and with individuals, he must be acting by means of its ordinary system, or by quickening, or as it were, stimulating its powers, or by superseding or inter-rupting it ; in other words, by means of what is called nature, or by miracle ; and whereas strictly miraculous interference must be, from the nature of the case, rare, it stands to reason that, unless He has simply retired, and has left the world ordinarily to itself,—content with having originally imposed on it certain general laws, which will for the most part work out the ends which He contemplates,—He is acting through, with, and beneath those physical, social, and moral laws, of which our experience informs us. Now it has ever been a firm article of Christian faith, that His Providence is in fact not general merely, but is, on the contrary, thus particular and personal ; and that, as there is a particular Providence, so of necessity that Providence is secretly concurring and co-operating with that system which meets the eye, and which is commonly recognized among men as existing. It is not too much to say that this is the one great rule on which the Divine Dispensations with mankind have been and are conducted, that the visible world is the instrument, yet the veil, of the world invisible,—the veil, yet still partially the symbol and index : so that all that exists or happens visibly, conceals and yet suggests, and above all subserves, a system of persons, facts, and events beyond itself.

Thus the course of things has a natural termination as well as a natural origin : it tends towards final causes while it springs from physical ; it is ever issuing from things which we see round about us ; it is ever passing on into what is matter of faith, not of sight. What is called and seems to be cause and effect, is rather an order of sequence, and does not preclude, nay, perhaps implies, the presence of unseen spiritual agency as its real author. This is the animating principle both of the Church's ritual and of Scripture interpretation ; in the latter it is the basis of the theory of the double sense ; in the former it makes ceremonies and observances to be signs, seals, means, and pledges of supernatural grace. It is the mystical principle in the one, it is the sacramental in the other. All that is seen,— the world, the Bible, the Church, the civil polity, and man himself,—are types, and, in their degree and place, representatives and organs of an unseen world, truer and higher than themselves. The only difference between them is, that some things bear their supernatural character upon their surface, are historically creations of the supernatural system, or are perceptibly instrumental, or obviously symbolical : while others rather seem to be complete in themselves, or run counter to the unseen system which they really subserve, and thereby make demands upon our faith.

This may be illustrated from the creation of man. The Creator " formed man of the dust of the ground, *and* breathed into his nostrils the breath of life, and man became a living soul." He first formed a material tabernacle, and then endued it with an unseen life. Now some philosophers, somewhat after the manner of the ancient Gnostics whom Mr. Milman mentions, have speculated on the probability of man's being originally of some brute nature, some vast mis-shapen lizard of the primeval period, which at length by the force of nature, from whatever secret causes, was exalted into a rational being, and gradually shaped its proportions and refined its properties by the influence of the rational principle which got possession of it. Such a theory is of course irreconcilable with the letter of the sacred text, to say no more ; but it bears an analogy, and at least supplies an illustration, to many facts and events which take place in this world. . . . When He would set up a divine polity, He takes a polity which already is, or one in course of forming. Nor does He interfere with its natural growth, development, or dependence on things visible. He does not shut it up in a desert, and there supply it with institutions unlike those which might naturally come to it from the contact and intercourse of the external world. He does but modify, quicken, or direct the powers of nature or the laws of society. . . .

★   ★   ★

The Israelitish polity had a beginning, a middle, and an end, like other things of time and place ; its captivities were the natural consequences, its monarchy was the natural expedient, of a state of political weakness. Its territory was a battle-ground, and its power was the alternate ally, of the rival empires of Egypt and Assyria. Heathen travellers may have surveyed the Holy Land, and have thought it but a narrow strip of Syria. So it was ; what then ? till the comparative anatomist can be said by his science to disprove the rationality and responsibility of man, the politician or geographer of this world does nothing, by dissertations in his own particular line of thought, towards quenching the secret light of Israel, or dispossessing its angelic guardians of the height of Sion or of the sepulchres of the prophets. Its history is twofold, worldly to the world, and heavenly to the heirs of heaven.

What is true of Judaism is true of Christianity. The kingdom of Christ, though not of this world, yet is in the world, and has a visible, material, social shape. It consists of men, and it has developed according to the laws under which combinations of men develop. It has an external aspect similar to all other kingdoms. We may generalize and include it as one among the various kinds of polity, as one among the empires, which have been upon the earth. It is called the fifth kingdom ; and as being numbered with the previous four which were earthly, it is thereby, in fact, compared with them. We may write its history, and make it look as like those which were before or contemporary with it, as a man is like a monkey. Now we come at length to Mr. Milman : this is what he has been doing. He has been viewing the history of the Church on the side of the world. Its rise from nothing, the gradual aggrandizement of its bishops, the consolidation of its polity and government, its relation to powers of the earth, its intercourse with foreign philosophies and religions, its conflict with external and internal enemies, the mutual action for good or for evil which has been carried on between it and foreign systems, political and intellectual, its large extension, its growth and resolution into a monarchy, its temporal greatness, its gradual divisions and decay, and the natural causes which operated throughout,— these are the subjects in which he delights, to which he has dedicated himself,—that is, as far as they can be detached from their directly religious bearing ; and unless readers understand this, they will think that what is but *a contemplation of what is outside*, is intended by him for *a denial of what is inside*. Whether such denial has in any measure resulted, even in Mr. Milman's own mind, from such contemplation, is a farther question, afterwards to be considered ; but, anyhow, it is to be feared, that too many persons will unfairly run away from his book with the notion that to ignore the Almighty in ecclesiastical history is really to deny Him.

Essays Critical and Historical II

B

We repeat, then, in perfect sincerity and much anxiety, our inquiry,—What tenet of Christianity will escape proscription, if the principle is once admitted, that a sufficient account is given of an opinion, and a sufficient ground for making light of it, as soon as it is historically referred to some human origin ? What will be our Christianity ? What shall we have to believe ? What will be left to us ? Will more remain than a *caput mortuum*, with no claim on our profession or devotion ? Will the Gospel be a substance ? Will Revelation have done more than introduce a *quality* into our moral life world, not anything that can be contemplated by itself, obeyed and per-petuated ? This we do verily believe to be the end of the speculations, of which Mr. Milman's volumes at least serve as an illustration. If we indulge them, Christianity will melt away in our hands like snow ; we shall be unbelievers before we at all suspect where we are. With a sigh we shall suddenly detect the real state of the case. We shall look on Christianity, not as a religion, but as a past event which exerted a great influence on the course of the world, when it happened, and gave a tone and direction to religion, government, philosophy, literature, manners ; an idea which developed itself in various directions strongly, which was indeed from the first materialized into a system or a church, and is still upheld as such by numbers, but by an error ; a great boon to the world, bestowed by the Giver of all good, as the discovery of printing may be, or the steam-engine, but as incapable of continuity, except in its effects, as the shock of an earthquake, or the impulsive force which commenced the motions of the planets.

Essays Critical and Historical II

C

Moreover, I can quite enter into the sentiment with which members of the liberal and infidel school investigate the history and the documents of the early Church. They profess a view of Christianity, truer than the world has ever had ; nor, on the assumption of their principles, is there anything shocking to good sense in this profession. They look upon the Christian Religion as something simply human ; and there is no reason at all why a phenomenon of that kind should not be better understood, in its origin and nature, as years proceed. It is, indeed, an intolerable paradox to assert, that a revelation, given from God to man, should lie unknown or mistaken for eighteen centuries, and now at length should be suddenly deciphered by individuals ; but it is quite intelligible to assert, and plausible to argue, that a human fact should be more philosophically explained than it was eighteen hundred years ago, and more exactly ascertained than it was a thousand. History is at this day undergoing a process of revolution ; the science of criticism, the disinterment of antiquities, the unrolling of manuscripts, the interpretation of inscriptions, have thrown us into a new world of thought ; characters and events come forth transformed in the process ; romance, prejudice, local tradition, party bias, are no longer accepted as guarantees of truth ; the order and mutual relation of events are readjusted ; the springs and the scope of action are reversed. Were Christianity a mere work of man, it, too, might turn out something different from what it has hitherto been considered ; its history might require re-writing, as the history of Rome, or of the earth's strata, or of languages, or of chemical action. A Catholic neither deprecates nor fears such inquiry, though he abhors the spirit in which it is too often conducted. He is willing that infidelity should do its work against the Church, knowing that she will be found just where she was, when the assault is over. It is nothing to him, though her enemies put themselves to the trouble of denying everything that has hitherto been taught, and begin with constructing her history all over again, for he is quite sure that they will end at length with a compulsory admission of what at first they so wantonly discarded.

Difficulties of Anglicans I

D

This is the great, manifest, historical phenomenon which converted me,—to which all particular inquiries converged.

Christianity is not a matter of opinion, but an external fact, entering into, carried out in, indivisible from, the history of the world. It has a bodily occupation of the world ; it is one continuous fact or thing, the same from first to last, distinct from everything else : to be a Christian is to partake of, to submit to, this thing ; and the simple question was, Where, what is this thing in this age, which in the first age was the Catholic Church ? The answer was undeniable ; the Church called Catholic now, is that very same thing in hereditary descent, in organization, in principles, in position, in external relations, which was called the Catholic Church then ; name and thing have ever gone together, by an uninterrupted connection and succession, from then till now. Whether it had been corrupted in its teaching was, at best, a matter of opinion. It was indefinitely more evident a fact, that it stood on the ground and in the place of the ancient Church, as its heir and representative, than that certain peculiarities in its teaching were really innovations and corruptions.

Difficulties of Anglicans I

WHAT THE AGE IS COMING TO

This is what the Age is coming to, and I wish it observed. We know it denies the existence of the Church as a divine institution : it denies that Christianity has been cast into any particular social mould. Well : but this, I say, is not all ; it is rapidly tending to deny the existence of any system of Christianity either ; any creed, doctrine, philosophy, or by whatever other name we designate it. Hitherto it had been usual, indeed, to give up the Church, and to speak only of the covenant, religion, creed, matter, or system of the Gospel ; to consider the Gospel as a sort of literature or philosophy, open for all to take and appropriate, not confined to any set of men, yet still a real, existing system of religion. This has been the approved line of opinion in our part of the world for the last hundred and fifty years ; but now a further step is about to be taken. The view henceforth is to be, that Christianity does not exist in documents, any more than in institutions ; in other words, the Bible will be given up as well as the Church. It will be said that the benefit which Christianity has done to the world, and which its Divine Author meant it should do, was to give an impulse to society, to infuse a spirit, to direct, control, purify, enlighten the mass of human thought and action, but not to be a separate and definite something, whether doctrine or association, existing objectively, integral, and with an identity, and for ever, and with a claim upon our homage and obedience. And all this fearfully coincides with the symptoms in other directions of the spread of a Pantheistic spirit, that is, the religion of beauty, imagination, and philosophy, without constraint moral or intellectual, a religion speculative and self-indulgent. Pantheism, indeed, is the great deceit which awaits the Age to come.

Discussions and Arguments

THE DANGER INVOLVED IN THE CULTIVATION
OF THE INTELLECT

The human mind, as you know, my Brethren, may be regarded from two principal points of view, as intellectual and as moral. As intellectual, it apprehends truth; as moral, it apprehends duty. The perfection of the intellect is called ability and talent; the perfection of our moral nature is virtue. And it is our great misfortune here, and our trial, that, as things are found in the world, the two are separated, and independent of each other; that, where power of intellect is, there need not be virtue; and that where right, and goodness, and moral greatness are, there need not be talent. It was not so in the beginning; not that our nature is essentially different from what it was when first created; but that the Creator, upon its creation, raised it above itself by a supernatural grace, which blended together all its faculties, and made them conspire into one whole, and act in common towards one end; so that, had the race continued in that blessed state of privilege, there never would have been distance, rivalry, hostility between one faculty and another. It is otherwise now; so much the worse for us;—the grace is gone; the soul cannot hold together; it falls to pieces; its elements strive with each other. . . .

This is a very serious state of things; and what makes it worse is, that these various faculties and powers of the human mind have so long been separated from each other, so long cultivated and developed each by itself, that it comes to be taken for granted that they cannot be united; and it is commonly thought, because some men follow duty, others pleasure, others glory, and others intellect, therefore that one of these things excludes the other; that duty cannot be pleasant, that virtue cannot be intellectual, that goodness cannot be great, that conscientiousness cannot be heroic; and the fact is often so, I grant, that there *is* a separation, though I deny its necessity. I grant, that, from the disorder and confusion into which the human mind has fallen, too often good men are not attractive, and bad men are; too often cleverness, or wit, or taste, or richness of fancy, or keenness of intellect, or depth, or know-ledge, or pleasantness and agreeableness, is on the side of error and not on the side of virtue. Excellence, as things are, does lie, I grant, in more directions than one, and it is ever easier to excel in one thing than in two. If then a man has more talent, there is the chance that he will have less goodness ; if he is careful about his religious duties, there is the chance he is behind-hand in general knowledge ; and in matter of fact, in particular cases, persons may be found, correct and virtuous, who are heavy, narrow-minded, and unintellectual, and again, unprincipled men, who are brilliant and amusing. And thus you see, my Brethren, how that particular temptation comes about, of which I speak, when boyhood is past, and youth is opening ;—not only is the soul plagued and tormented by the thousand temptations which rise up within it, but it is exposed moreover to the sophistry of the Evil One, whispering that duty and religion are very right indeed, admirable, supernatural, —who doubts it ?—but that, somehow or other, religious people are commonly either very dull or very tiresome : nay, that religion itself after all is more suitable to women and children, who live at home, than to men.

O my Brethren, do you not confess to the truth of much of what I have been saying ? Is it not so, that, when your mind began to open, in proportion as it opened, it was by that very opening made rebellious against what you knew to be duty ? In matter of fact, was not your intellect in league with dis-obedience ? Instead of uniting knowledge and religion, as you might have done, did you not set one against the other ? . . .

[The youth] has aspirations and ambitions which home does not satisfy. He wants more than home can give. His curiosity now takes a new turn ; he listens to views and discussions which are inconsistent with the sanctity of religious faith. At first he has no temptation to adopt them ; only he wishes to know what is " said." As times goes on, however, living with companions who have no fixed principle, and who, if they do not oppose, at least do not take for granted, any of the most elementary truths ; or worse, hearing or reading what is directly against religion, at length, without being conscious of it, he admits a sceptical influence upon his mind. He does not know it, he does not recognize it, but there it is ; and, *before* he recognizes it, it leads him to a fretful, impatient way of speaking of the persons, conduct, words, and measures of religious men or of men in authority. This is the way in which he relieves his mind of the burden which is growing heavier and heavier every day. And so he goes on, approximating more and more closely to sceptics and infidels, and feeling more and more congeniality with their modes of thinking, till some day suddenly, from some accident, the facts break upon him, and he sees clearly that he is an unbeliever himself.

He can no longer conceal from himself that he does not believe, and a sharp anguish darts through him, and for a time he is made miserable ; next, he *laments* indeed that former undoubting faith, which he has lost, but as some pleasant dream ;—a dream, though a pleasant one, from which he has been awakened, but which, however pleasant, *he* forsooth, cannot help *being* a dream. And his next stage is to experience a great expansion and elevation of mind ; for his field of view is swept clear of all that filled it from childhood, and now he may build up for himself anything he pleases instead. So he begins to form his own ideas of things, and these please and satisfy him for a time ; then he gets used to them, and tires of them, and he takes up others ; and now he has begun that everlasting round of seeking and never finding : at length, after various trials, he gives up the search altogether, and decides that nothing can be known, and there is no such thing as truth, and that if anything is to be professed, the creed he started from is as good as any other, and has more claims ;—however, that really nothing is true, nothing is certain. Or, if he be of a more ardent temperature, or, like Augustine, the object of God's special mercy, then he cannot give up the inquiry, though he has no chance of solving it, and he roams about, " walking through dry places, seeking rest, and finding none." . . .

Now, my Brethren, observe, the strength of this delusion lies in there being a sort of truth in it. Young men feel a consciousness of certain faculties within them which demand exercise, aspirations which must have an object, for which they do not commonly find exercise or object in religious circles. This want is no excuse for them, if they think, say, or do anything against faith or morals : but still it is the occasion of their sinning. It is the fact, they are not only moral, they are intellectual beings ; but, ever since the fall of man, religion is here, and philosophy is there ; each has its own centres of influence, separate from the other ; intellectual men desiderate something in the homes of religion, and religious men desiderate something in the schools of science.

Here, then, I conceive, is the object of the Holy See and the Catholic Church in setting up Universities ; it is to reunite things which were in the beginning joined together by God, and have been put asunder by man. Some persons will say that I am thinking of confining, distorting, and stunting the growth of the intellect by ecclesiastical supervision. I have no such thought. Nor have I any thought of a compromise, as if religion must give up something, and science something. I wish the intellect to range with the utmost freedom, and religion to enjoy an equal freedom ; but what I am stipulating for is, that they should be found in one and the same place, and exemplified in the same persons. I want to destroy that diversity of centres, which puts everything into confusion by creating a contrariety of influences. I wish the same spots and the same individuals to be at once oracles of philosophy and shrines of devotion. It will not satisfy me, what satisfies so many, to have two independent systems, intellectual and religious, going at once side by side, by a sort of division of labour, and only accidentally brought together. It will not satisfy me, if religion is here, and science there, and young men converse with science all day, and lodge with religion in the evening. It is not touching the evil, to which these remarks have been directed, if young men eat and drink and sleep in one place, and think in another : I want the same roof to contain both the intellectual and the moral discipline. Devotion is not a sort of finish given to the sciences ; nor is science a sort of feather in the cap, if I may so express myself, an ornament and a set-off to devotion. I want the intellectual layman to be religious, and the devout ecclesiastic to be intellectual.

Sermons on Various Occasions

THE METHOD OF THEOLOGY IN CONTRAST
WITH THAT OF SCIENCE

Induction is the instrument of Physics, and deduction only is the instrument of Theology. There the simple question is, What is revealed? all doctrinal knowledge flows from one fountain head. If we are able to enlarge our view and multiply our propositions, it must be merely by the comparison and adjustment of the original truths; if we would solve new questions, it must be by consulting old answers. The notion of doctrinal knowledge absolutely novel, and of simple addition from without, is intolerable to Catholic ears, and never was entertained by any one who was even approaching to an understanding of our creed. Revelation is all in all in doctrine; the Apostles its sole depository, the inferential method its sole instrument, and ecclesiastical authority its sole sanction. The Divine Voice has spoken once for all, and the only question is about its meaning. Now this process, as far as it was reasoning, was the very mode of reasoning which, as regards physical knowledge, the school of Bacon has superseded by the inductive method :—no wonder, then, that that school should be irritated and indignant to find that a subject-matter remains still, in which their favourite instrument has no office; no wonder that they rise up against this memorial of an antiquated system, as an eyesore and an insult; and no wonder that the very force and dazzling success of their own method in its own departments should sway or bias unduly the religious sentiments of any persons who come under its influence. They assert that no new truth can be gained by deduction; Catholics assent, but add that, as regards religious truth, they have not to seek at all, for they have it already. Christian Truth is purely of revelation; that revelation we can but explain, we cannot increase, except relatively to our own apprehensions; without it we should have known nothing of its contents, with it we know just as much as its contents, and nothing more. And, as it was given by a divine act independent of man, so will it remain in spite of man. Niebuhr may revolutionize history,

Lavoisier chemistry, Newton astronomy ; but God Himself is the author as well as the subject of theology. When Truth can change, its Revelation can change ; when human reason can outreason the Omniscient, then may it supersede His work.

The Idea of a University

B

I observe, then, that the elementary methods of reasoning and inquiring used in Theology and Physics are contrary the one to the other ; each of them has a method of its own ; and in this, I think, has lain the point of controversy between the two schools, viz., that neither of them has been quite content to remain on its own homestead, but that, whereas each has its own method, which is the best for its own science, each has considered it the best for all purposes whatever, and has at different times thought to impose it upon the other science, to the disparagement or rejection of that opposite method which legitimately belongs to it.

The argumentative method of Theology is that of a strict science, such as Geometry, or deductive ; the method of Physics, at least on starting, is that of an empirical pursuit, or inductive. This peculiarity on either side arises from the nature of the case. In Physics a vast and omnigenous mass of information lies before the inquirer, all in a confused litter, and needing arrangement and analysis. In Theology such varied phenomena are wanting, and Revelation presents itself instead. What is known in Christianity is just that which is revealed, and nothing more ; certain truths, communicated directly from above, are committed to the keeping of the faithful, and to the very last nothing can really be added to those truths. From the time of the Apostles to the end of the world no strictly new truth can be added to the theological information which the Apostles were inspired to deliver. It is possible of course to make numberless deductions from the original doctrines ; but, as the conclusion is ever in its premisses, such deductions are not, strictly speaking, an addition ; and, though experience may variously guide and modify those deductions, still, on the whole, Theology retains the severe character of a science, advancing syllogistically from premisses to conclusion.

The method of Physics is just the reverse of this : it has hardly any principles or truths to start with, externally delivered and already ascertained. It has to commence with sight and touch ; it has to handle, weigh, and measure its own exuberant *sylva* of phenomena, and from these to advance to new truths,—truths, that is, which are beyond and distinct from the phenomena from which they originate. Thus Physical Science is experimental, Theology traditional ; Physical Science is the richer, Theology the more exact ; Physics the bolder, Theology the surer ; Physics progressive, Theology, in comparison, stationary ; Theology is loyal to the past, Physics has visions of the future. Such they are, I repeat, and such their respective methods of inquiry, from the nature of the case.

Ibid.

THE INTIMATIONS OF CONSCIENCE IN CONTRAST WITH THOSE OF SCIENCE

You will observe, then, Gentlemen, that those higher sciences of which I have spoken, Morals and Religion, are not represented to the intelligence of the world by intimations and notices strong and obvious, such as those which are the foundation of Physical Science. The physical nature lies before us, patent to the sight, ready to the touch, appealing to the senses in so unequivocal a way that the science which is founded upon it is as real to us as the fact of our personal existence. But the phenomena, which are the basis of morals and Religion, have nothing of this luminous evidence. Instead of being obtruded upon our notice, so that we cannot possibly overlook them, they are the dictates either of Conscience or of Faith. They are faint shadows and tracings, certain indeed, but delicate, fragile, and almost evanescent, which the mind recognizes at one time, not at another,—discerns when it is calm, loses when it is in agitation. The reflection of sky and mountains in the lake is a proof that sky and mountains are around it, but the twilight, or the mist, or the sudden storm hurries away the beautiful image, which leaves behind it no memorial of what it was. Something like this are the Moral Law and the informations of Faith, as they present themselves to individual minds. Who can deny the existence of Conscience ? who does not feel the force of its injunctions ? but how dim is the illumination in which it is invested, and how feeble its influence, compared with that evidence of sight and touch which is the foundation of Physical Science ! How easily can we be talked out of our clearest views of duty ! how does this or that moral precept crumble into nothing when we rudely handle it ! how does the fear of sin pass off from us, as quickly as the glow of modesty dies away from the countenance ! and then we say, " It is all superstition." However, after a time we look round, and then to our surprise we see, as before, the same law of duty, the same moral precepts, the same protests against sin, appearing over against us, in their old places, as if they never had been brushed away, like the divine handwriting upon the wall at the banquet. Then perhaps we approach them rudely, and inspect them irreverently, and accost them sceptically, and away they go again, like so many spectres,—shining in their cold beauty, but not presenting themselves bodily to us, for our inspection, so to say, of their hands and their feet. And thus these awful, supernatural, bright, majestic, delicate apparitions, much as we may in our hearts acknowledge their sovereignty, are no match as a foundation of Science for the hard, palpable, material facts which make up the province of Physics. . . . Such, I say, is the natural condition of mankind :—we depend upon a seat of government which is in another world ; we are directed and governed by intimations from above ; we need a local government on earth.

That great institution, then, the Catholic Church, has been set up by Divine Mercy, as a present, visible antagonist, and the only possible antagonist, to sight and sense. Conscience, reason, good feeling, the instincts of our moral nature, the traditions of Faith, the conclusions and deductions of philosophical religion, are no match at all for the stubborn facts (for they *are* facts, though there are other facts besides them), for the facts, which are the foundation of physical, and in particular of medical, science. Gentlemen, if you feel, as you must feel, the whisper of a law of moral truth within you, and the impulse to believe, be sure there is nothing whatever on earth which can be the sufficient champion of these sovereign authorities of your soul, which can vindicate and preserve them to you, and make you loyal to them, but the Catholic Church. You fear they will go, you see with dismay that they are going, under the continual impression created on your mind by the details of the material science to which you have devoted your lives. It is so—I do not deny it ; except under rare and happy circumstances, go they will, unless you have Catholicism to back you up in keeping faithful to them. The world is a rough antagonist of spiritual truth : sometimes with mailed hand, sometimes with pertinacious logic, sometimes with a storm of irresistible facts, it presses on against you. What it says is true perhaps as far as it goes, but it is not the whole truth, or the most important truth. These more important truths, which the natural heart admits in their substance, though it cannot maintain,—the being of a God, the certainty of future retribution, the claims of the moral law, the reality of sin, the hope of supernatural help,—of these the Church is in matter of fact the undaunted and the only defender.

The Idea of a University

THE PHILOSOPHY OF AN IMPERIAL
INTELLECT

And here, Gentlemen, we recognize the special character of the Philosophy I am speaking of, if Philosophy it is to be called, in contrast with the method of a strict science or system. Its teaching is not founded on one idea, or reducible to certain formulæ. Newton might discover the great law of motion in the physical world, and the key to ten thousand phenomena ; and a similar resolution of complex facts into simple principles may be possible in other departments of nature ; but the great Universe itself, moral and material, sensible and supernatural, cannot be gauged and meted by even the greatest of human intellects, and its constituent parts admit indeed of comparison and adjustment, but not of fusion. This is the point which bears directly on the subject which I set before me when I began, and towards which I am moving in all I have said or shall be saying.

I observe, then, and ask you, Gentlemen, to bear in mind, that the philosophy of an imperial intellect, for such I am considering a University to be, is based, not so much on simplification as on discrimination. Its true representative defines, rather than analyzes. He aims at no complete catalogue, or interpretation of the subjects of knowledge, but a following out, as far as man can, what in its fulness is mysterious and unfathomable. Taking into his charge all sciences, methods, collections of facts, principles, doctrines, truths, which are the reflexions of the universe upon the human intellect, he admits them all, he disregards none, and, as disregarding none, he allows none to exceed or encroach. His watchword is, Live and let live. He takes things as they are ; he submits to them all, as far as they go ; he recognizes the insuperable lines of demarcation which run between subject and subject ; he observes how separate truths lie relatively to each other, where they concur, where they part company, and where, being carried too far, they cease to be truths at all. It is his office to determine how much can be known in each province of thought ; when we must be contented not to know ; in what direction inquiry is hopeless, or on the other hand full of promise ; where it gathers into coils insoluble by reason, where it is absorbed in mysteries, or runs into the abyss. It will be his care to be familiar with the signs of real and apparent difficulties, with the methods proper to particular subject-matters, what in each particular case are the limits of a rational scepticism, and what the claims of a peremptory faith. If he has one cardinal maxim in his philosophy, it is, that truth cannot be contrary to truth ; if he has a second, it is, that truth often *seems* contrary to truth ; and, if a third, it is the practical conclusion, that we must be patient with such appearances, and not be hasty to pronounce them to be really of a more formidable character.

It is the very immensity of the system of things, the human record of which he has in charge, which is the reason of this patience and caution ; for that immensity suggests to him that the contrarieties and mysteries, which meet him in the various sciences, may be simply the consequences of our necessarily defective comprehension. There is but one thought greater than that of the universe, and that is the thought of its Maker. If, Gentlemen, for one single instant, leaving my proper train of thought, I allude to our knowledge of the Supreme Being, it is in order to deduce from it an illustration bearing upon my subject. He, though One, is a sort of world of worlds in Himself, giving birth in our minds to an indefinite number of distinct truths, each ineffably more mysterious than any thing that is found in this universe of space and time. Any one of His attributes, considered by itself, is the object of an inexhaustible science : and the attempt to reconcile any two or three of them together,—love, power, justice, sanctity, truth, wisdom,—affords matter for an everlasting controversy. We are able to apprehend and receive each divine attribute in its elementary form, but still we are not able to accept them in their infinity, either in themselves or in union with each other. Yet we do not deny the first because it cannot be perfectly reconciled with the second, nor the second because it is in apparent contrariety with the first and the third. The case is the same in its degree with His creation material and moral. It is the highest wisdom to accept truth of whatever kind, wherever it is clearly ascertained to be such, though there be difficulty in adjusting it with other known truth.

The Idea of a University

A FORM OF INFIDELITY OF THE DAY

Though it cannot be denied that at the present day, in consequence of the close juxtaposition and intercourse of men of all religions, there is a considerable danger of the subtle, silent, unconscious perversion and corruption of Catholic intellects, who as yet profess, and sincerely profess, their submission to the authority of Revelation, still that danger is far inferior to what it was in one portion of the middle ages. Nay, contrasting the two periods together, we may even say, that in this very point they differ, that, in the medieval, since Catholicism was then the sole religion recognized in Christendom, unbelief necessarily made its advances under the language and the guise of faith ; whereas in the present, when universal toleration prevails, and it is open to assail revealed truth . . . unbelief in consequence throws off the mask, and takes up a position over against us in citadels of its own, and confronts us in the broad light and with a direct assault. And I have no hesitation in saying (apart of course from moral and ecclesiastical considerations, and under correction of the command and policy of the Church), that I prefer to live in an age when the fight is in the day, not in the twilight ; and think it a gain to be speared by a foe, rather than to be stabbed by a friend.

I do not, then, repine at all at the open development of unbelief in Germany, supposing unbelief is to be, or at its growing audacity in England ; not as if I were satisfied with the state of things, considered positively, but because, in the unavoidable alternative of avowed unbelief and secret, my own personal leaning is in favour of the former. I hold that unbelief is in some shape unavoidable in an age of intellect and in a world like this, considering that faith requires an act of the will, and presupposes the due exercise of religious advantages. You may persist in calling Europe Catholic, though it is not ; you may enforce an outward acceptance of Catholic dogma, and an outward obedience to Catholic precept ; and your enactments may be, so far, not only pious in themselves, but even merciful towards the teachers of false doctrine, as well as just towards their victims ; but this is all that you can do ; you cannot bespeak conclusions which, in spite of yourselves, you are leaving free to the human will. There will be, I say, in spite of you, unbelief and immorality to the end of the world, and you must be prepared for immorality more odious, and unbelief more astute, more subtle, more bitter, and more resentful, in proportion as it is obliged to dissemble.

It is one great advantage of an age in which unbelief speaks out, that Faith can speak out too ; that, if falsehood assails Truth, Truth can assail falsehood. In such an age it is possible to found a University more emphatically Catholic than could be set up in the middle age, because Truth can entrench itself carefully, and define its own profession severely, and display its colours unequivocally, by occasion of that very unbelief which so shamelessly vaunts itself. And a kindred advantage to this is the confidence which, in such an age, we can place in all who are around us, so that we need look for no foes but those who are in the enemy's camp.

* * *

In this day . . . Truth and Error lie over against each other with a valley between them, and David goes forward in the sight of all men, and from his own camp, to engage with the Philistine. Such is the providential overruling of that principle of toleration, which was conceived in the spirit of unbelief, in order to the destruction of Catholicity. The sway of the Church is contracted ; but she gains in intensity what she loses in extent. She has now a direct command and a reliable influence over her own institutions, which was wanting in the middle ages. A University is her possession in these times, as well as her creation : nor has she the need, which once was so urgent, to expel heresies from her pale, which have now their own centres of attraction elsewhere, and spontaneously take their departure. Secular advantages no longer present an inducement to hypocrisy, and her members in consequence have the consolation of being able to be sure of each other. . . . I repeat it, I would rather fight with unbelief as we find it in the nineteenth century, than as it existed in the twelfth and thirteenth.

I look out, then, into the enemy's camp, and I try to trace the outlines of the hostile movements and the preparations for assault which are there in agitation against us. The arming and the manœuvring, the earth-works and the mines, go on incessantly ; and one cannot of course tell, without the gift of prophecy, which of his projects will be carried into effect and attain its purpose, and which will eventually fail or be abandoned. Threatening demonstrations may come to nothing ; and those who are to be our most formidable foes, may before the attack elude our observation. All these uncertainties, we know, are the lot of the soldier in the field : and they are parallel to those which befall the warriors of the Temple. Fully feeling the force of such considerations, and under their correction, nevertheless I make my anticipations according to the signs of the times ; and such must be my *proviso*, when I proceed to describe some characteristics of one particular form of infidelity, which is coming into existence and activity over against us, in the intellectual citadels of England.

It must not be supposed that I attribute, what I am going to speak of as a form of infidelity of the day, to any given individual or individuals ; nor is it necessary to my purpose to suppose that any one man as yet consciously holds, or sees the drift of, that portion of the theory to which he has given assent. I am to describe a set of opinions which may be considered as the true explanation of many floating views, and the converging point of a multitude of separate and independent minds ; and, as of old Arius or Nestorius not only was spoken of in his own person, but was viewed as the abstract and typical teacher of the heresy which he introduced, and thus his name denoted a heretic more complete and explicit, even though not more formal, than the heresiarch himself, so here too, in like manner, I may be describing a school of thought in its fully developed proportions, which at present every one, to whom membership with it is imputed, will at once begin to disown, and I may be pointing to teachers whom no one will be able to descry. Still it is not less true that I may be speaking of tendencies and elements which exist, and he may come in person at last, who comes at first to us merely in his spirit and in his power.

* * *

I have already said that its fundamental dogma is, that nothing can be known for certain about the unseen world. This being taken for granted as a self-evident point, undeniable as soon as stated, it goes on, or will go on, to argue that, in consequence, the immense outlay which has been made of time, anxiety, and toil, of health, bodily and mental, upon theological researches, has been simply thrown away ; nay, has been, not useless merely, but even mischievous, inasmuch as it has indirectly thwarted the cultivation of studies of far greater promise and of an evident utility. This is the main position of the School I am contemplating ; and the result, in the minds of its members, is a deep hatred and a bitter resentment against the Power which has managed, as they consider, to stunt the world's knowledge and the intellect of man for so many hundred years. Thus much I have already said, and now I am going to state the line of policy which these people will adopt, and the course of thought which that policy of theirs will make necessary to them or natural.

Supposing, then, it is the main tenet of the School in question, that the study of Religion as a science has been the bane of philosophy and knowledge, what remedy will its masters apply for the evils they deplore ? Should they profess themselves the antagonists of theology, and engage in argumentative exercises with theologians ? This evidently would be to increase, to perpetuate the calamity. Nothing, they will say to themselves, do religious men desire so ardently, nothing would so surely advance the cause of Religion, as Controversy. The very policy of religious men, they will argue, is to get the world to fix its attention steadily upon the subject of Religion, and Controversy is the most effectual means of doing this. And their own game, they will consider, is, on the contrary, to be elaborately silent about it. Should they then not go on to shut up the theological schools, and exclude Religion from the subjects scientifically treated in philosophical education ?

This indeed has been, and is, a favourite mode of proceeding with very many of the enemies of Theology ; but still it cannot be said to have been justified by any greater success than the policy of Controversy. . . . Whatever be the real value of Religion, say these philosophers to themselves, it has a name in the world, and must not be ill-treated, lest men should rally round it from a feeling of generosity. They will decide, in consequence, that the exclusive method, though it has met with favour in this generation, is quite as much a mistake as the controversial.

Turning, then, to the Universities of England, they will pronounce that the true policy to be observed there would be simply to let the Schools of Theology alone. Most unfortunate it is that they have been roused from the state of decadence and torpor in which they lay some twenty or thirty years ago. . . . However, the mischief has been done ; and now the wisest course for the interests of infidelity is to leave it to itself, and let the fever gradually subside ; treatment would but irritate it. Not to interfere with Theology, not to raise a little finger against it, is the only means of superseding it. The more bitter is the hatred which such men bear it, the less they must show it.

What, then, is the line of action which they must pursue ? They think, and rightly think, that, in all contests, the wisest and largest policy is to conduct a positive, not a negative opposition, not to prevent but to anticipate, to obstruct by constructing, and to exterminate by supplanting. To cast any slight upon Theology, whether in its Protestant or its Catholic schools, would be to elicit an inexhaustible stream of polemics, and a phalanx of dogmatic doctors and confessors. . . .

The proper procedure, then, is not to oppose Theology, but to rival it. Leave its teachers to themselves ; merely aim at the introduction of other studies, which, while they have the accidental charm of novelty, possess a surpassing interest, richness, and practical value of their own. Get possession of these studies, and appropriate them, and monopolize the use of them, to the exclusion of the votaries of Religion. Take it for granted, and protest, for the future, that Religion has nothing to do with the studies to which I am alluding, nor those studies with Religion. Exclaim and cry out, if the

Catholic Church presumes herself to handle what you mean to use as a weapon against her. The range of the Experimental Sciences, viz., psychology, and politics, and political economy, and the many departments of physics, various both in their subject-matter and their method of research ; the great Sciences which are the characteristics of this era, and which become the more marvellous, the more thoroughly they are understood,— astronomy, magnetism, chemistry, geology, comparative anatomy, natural history, ethnology, languages, political geography, antiquities,—these be your indirect but effectual means of overturning Religion ! They do but need to be seen in order to be pursued ; you will put an end, in the Schools of learning, to the long reign of the unseen shadowy world, by the mere exhibition of the visible. This was impossible heretofore, for the visible world was so little known itself ; but now, thanks to the New Philosophy, sight is able to contest the field with faith. The medieval philosopher had no weapon against Revelation but Metaphysics ; Physical Science has a better temper, if not a keener edge, for the purpose.

Now here I interrupt the course of thought I am tracing, to introduce a *caveat*, lest I should be thought to cherish any secret disrespect towards the sciences I have enumerated, or apprehension of their legitimate tendencies ; whereas my very object is to protest against a monopoly of them by others. And it is not surely a heavy imputation on them to say that they, as other divine gifts, may be used to wrong purposes, with which they have no natural connection, and for which they were never intended ; and that, as in Greece the element of beauty, with which the universe is flooded, and the poetical faculty, which is its truest interpreter, were made to minister to sensuality ; as, in the middle ages, abstract speculation, another great instrument of truth, was often frittered away in sophistical exercises ; so now, too, the department of fact, and the method of research and experiment which is proper to it, may for the moment eclipse the light of faith in the imagination of the student, and be degraded into the accidental tool, *hic et nunc*, of infidelity. I am as little hostile to physical science as I am to poetry or metaphysics ; but I wish for studies of every kind a legitimate application : nor do I grudge them to anti-Catholics, so that anti-Catholics will not claim to monopolize them, cry out when we profess them, or direct them against Revelation.

I wish, indeed, I could think that these studies were not intended by a certain school of philosophers to bear directly against its authority. There are those who hope, there are those who are sure, that in the incessant investigation of facts, physical, political, and moral, something or other, or many things, will sooner or later turn up, and stubborn facts too, simply contradictory of revealed declarations. . . . They imagine that the eternal, immutable word of God is to quail and come to nought before the penetrating intellect of man. And, where this feeling exists, there will be a still stronger motive for letting Theology alone. That party, with whom success is but a matter of time, can afford to wait patiently ; and if an inevitable train is laid for blowing up the fortress, why need we be anxious that the catastrophe should take place to-day, rather than to-morrow ?

But, without making too much of their own anticipations on this point, which may or may not be in part fulfilled, these men have secure grounds for knowing that the sciences, as they would pursue them, will at least be prejudicial to the religious sentiment. Any one study, of whatever kind, exclusively pursued, deadens in the mind the interest, nay, the perception of any other. . . . Specimens of this peculiarity occur every day. You can hardly persuade some men to talk about any thing but their own pursuit ; they refer the whole world to their own centre, and measure all matters by their own rule. . . . And in like manner it is clear that the tendency of science is to make men indifferentists or sceptics, merely by being exclusively pursued. The party, then, of whom I speak, understanding this well, would suffer disputations in the theological schools every day in the year, provided they can manage to keep the students of science at a distance from them.

Nor is this all ; they trust to the influence of the modern sciences on what may be called the Imagination. When any thing, which comes before us, is very unlike what we commonly experience, we consider it on that account untrue ; not because it really shocks our reason as improbable, but because it startles our imagination as strange. Now, Revelation presents to us a perfectly different aspect of the universe from that presented by the Sciences. The two informations are like the distinct subjects represented by the lines of the same drawing, which, accordingly as they are read on their concave or convex side, exhibit to us now a group of trees with branches and leaves, and now human faces hid amid the leaves, or some majestic figures standing out from the branches. Thus is faith opposed to sight : it is parallel to the contrast afforded by plane astronomy and physical ; plane, in accordance with our senses, discourses of the sun's rising and setting, while physical, in accordance with our reason, asserts, on the contrary, that the sun is all but stationary, and that it is the earth that moves. This is what is meant by saying that truth lies in a well ; phenomena are no measure of fact ; *primâ facie* representations, which we receive from without, do not reach to the real state of things, or put them before us simply as they are.

While, then, Reason and Revelation are consistent in fact, they often are inconsistent in appearance ; and this seeming discordance acts most keenly and alarmingly on the Imagination, and may suddenly expose a man to the temptation, and even hurry him on to the commission, of definite acts of unbelief, in which reason itself really does not come into exercise at all. I mean, let a person devote himself to the studies of the day ; let him be taught by the astronomer that our sun is but one of a million central luminaries, and our earth but one of ten million globes moving in space ; let him learn from the geologist that on that globe of ours enormous revolutions have been in progress through innumerable ages ; let him be told by the comparative anatomist of the minutely arranged system of organized nature ; by the chemist and physicist, of the peremptory yet intricate laws to which nature, organized and inorganic, is subjected ; by the ethnologist, of the originals, and ramifications, and varieties, and fortunes of nations ; by the antiquarian, of old cities disinterred, and primitive countries laid bare, with the specific forms of human society once existing ; by the linguist, of the slow formation and development of languages ; by the psychologist, the physiologist, and the economist, of the subtle, complicated structure of the breathing, energetic, restless world of men ; I say, let him take in and master the vastness of the view thus afforded him of Nature, its infinite complexity, its awful comprehensiveness, and its diversified yet harmonious colouring ; and then, when he has for years drank in and fed upon this vision, let him turn round to peruse the inspired records, or listen to the authoritative teaching of Revelation, the book of Genesis, or the warnings and prophecies of the Gospels, or the Symbolum *Quicumque,* or the Life of St. Antony or St. Hilarion, and he may certainly experience a most distressing revulsion of feeling,—not that his reason really deduces any thing from his much loved studies contrary to the faith, but that his imagination is bewildered, and swims with the sense of the ineffable distance of that faith from the view of things which is familiar to him, with its strangeness, and then again its rude simplicity, as he considers it, and its apparent poverty contrasted with the exuberant life and reality of his own world. All this, the school I am speaking of understands well ; it comprehends that, if it can but exclude the professors of Religion from the lecture-halls of science, it may safely allow them full play in their own ; for it will be able to rear up infidels, without speaking a word, merely by the terrible influence of that faculty against which both Bacon and Butler so solemnly warn us.

I say, it leaves the theologian the full and free possession of his own schools, for it thinks he will have no chance of arresting the opposite teaching or of rivalling the fascination of modern science. Knowing little, and caring less for the depth and largeness of that heavenly Wisdom, on which the Apostle delights to expatiate, or the variety of those sciences, dogmatic or ethical, mystical or hagiological, historical or exegetical, which Revelation has created, these philosophers know perfectly well that, in matter of fact, to beings, constituted as we are, sciences which concern this world and this state of existence are worth far more, are more arresting and attractive, than those which relate to a system of things which they do not see and cannot master by their natural powers. Sciences which deal with tangible facts, practical results, evergrowing discoveries, and perpetual novelties, which feed curiosity, sustain attention, and stimulate expectation, require, they consider, but a fair stage and no favour to distance that Ancient Truth, which never changes and but cautiously advances, in the race for popularity and power. And therefore they look out for the day when they shall have put down Religion, not by shutting its schools, but by emptying them ; not by disputing its tenets, but by the superior worth and persuasiveness of their own.

Such is the tactic which a new school of philosophers adopt against Christian Theology. They have this characteristic, compared with former schools of infidelity, viz., the union of intense hatred with a large toleration of Theology. They are professedly civil to it, and run a race with it. They rely, not on any logical disproof of it, but on three considerations ; first, on the effects of studies of whatever kind to indispose the mind towards other studies ; next, on the special effect of modern sciences upon the imagination, prejudicial to revealed truth ; and lastly, on the absorbing interest attached to those sciences from their marvellous results. This line of action will be forced upon these persons by the peculiar character and position of Religion in England.

The Idea of a University

LIBERALISM IN THE EIGHTEEN-SIXTIES

A

In our own day [the Church of England] contains three strong parties, revivals respectively of the three principles of religion, which from the first, in one shape or other, have exhibited themselves in its history : the Catholic, the Protestant, and the Sceptical ; each of them, it is hardly necessary to say, fiercely opposed to the other two.

First, the Apostolical or Tractarian party, which at present goes further in the direction of Catholicism than at any former time, or under any former manifestation ; so much so, that, in the instance of its more advanced adherents, it may be said to differ in nothing from Catholics, except in the doctrine of the Pope's Supremacy. This school arose in the 17th century, in the court of James I, and Charles I ; it was almost extinguished by the principles of Locke, and by the accession of William III, and of the House of Hanover. Its principles were silently taught and handed down through the 18th century by the non-jurors ; a sect of learned and zealous men who split off from the Church of England, with an Episcopal succession, when they were called on to take the oath of allegiance to William III ; and it has revived in our own day in a large and spreading party in the Church of England, by means of that movement, commenced in the TRACTS FOR THE TIMES (hence called Tractarian), of which so much is said in the present volume.

Secondly, the Evangelical party, which is the life of the Bible Societies through the world, and of most of the Protestant Missionary Societies. This party may be said to have begun in the Puritans, who first showed themselves in the last years of the reign of Queen Elizabeth ; it was well-nigh cast out of the Church of England, on the restoration of Charles II, in 1660. It took refuge among the dissenters from that Church, and was gradually expiring, when its doctrines revived with great success by means of the celebrated preachers, Whitefield and Wesley, both Anglican clergymen, who founded the influential sect of the Methodists. At the same time that they formed a sect external to the Established Church, they exerted an important influence in that Church itself, and developed gradually in it the Evangelical party, who are at present far the most powerful of the three schools which we are engaged in enumerating.

Thirdly, the Liberal party, in former centuries called by the less honourable name of Latitudinarian. It rose out of the quasi-Catholic or court party of Charles I's reign, and was fostered and spread by the introduction into England of the principles of Grotius and of the Arminians of Holland. The philosophy of Locke has already been mentioned as acting in the same direction. It took the part of the Revolution of 1688, and stood by the Whigs, by William III, and by the House of Hanover. The genius of its principles is averse to display or proselytism ; and though it has had conspicuous writers among Anglican divines, it has not numbered many followers till the last ten years, when, irritated by the success of the Tractarians, taking advantage of the conversion to Rome of some of their principal men, and aided by the importation into England of German literature, it has suddenly come forward on the public stage, and has propagated itself with such wonderful rapidity among the educated classes, that it would seem as if, in the next generation, the religious world will be divided between Deists and Catholics. Indeed its principles and modes of reasoning do not stop even at Deism.

Apologia (Note for French translation)

B

Distinct as are the liberal and Catholicizing parties in the Anglican Church both in their principles and their policy, it must not be supposed that they are also as distinct in the members that compose them. No line of demarcation can be drawn between the one collection of men and the other, in fact ; for no two minds are altogether alike ; and individually, Anglicans have each his own shade of opinion, and belong partly to this school, partly to that. Or rather, there is a large body of men who are neither the one nor the other ; they cannot be called an intermediate party, for they have no discriminating watchwords ; they range from those who are almost Catholic to those who are almost Liberals. They are not Liberals, because they do not glory in a state of doubt ; they cannot profess to be " Anglo-Catholics," because they are not prepared to give an internal assent to all that is put forth by the Church as truth of revelation. These are the men who, if they could, would unite old ideas with new ; who cannot give up tradition, yet are loth to shut the door to progress ; who look for a more exact adjustment of faith with reason than has hitherto been attained ; who love the conclusions of Catholic theology better than the proofs, and the methods of modern thought better than its results ; and who, in the present wide unsettlement of religious opinion, believe indeed, or wish to believe, Scripture and orthodox doctrine, taken as a whole, and cannot get themselves to avow any deliberate dissent from any part of either, but still, not knowing how to defend their belief with logical exactness, or at least feeling that there are large unsatisfied objections lying against parts of it, or having misgivings lest there should be such, acquiesce in what is called a practical belief, that is, accept revealed truths, only because such acceptance of them is the safest course, because they are probable, and because to hold them in consequence is a duty, not as if they felt absolutely certain, though they will not allow themselves to be actually in doubt. Such is about the description to be given of them as a class ; though, as we have said, they so materially differ from each other, that no general account of them will apply strictly to any individual in their body.

Discussions and Arguments

THE WORLD AND THE CATHOLIC CHURCH

Starting then with the being of a God, (which, as I have said, is as certain to me as the certainty of my own existence, though when I try to put the grounds of that certainty into logical shape I find a difficulty in doing so in mood and figure to my satisfaction), I look out of myself into the world of men, and there I see a sight which fills me with unspeakable distress. The world seems simply to give the lie to that great truth, of which my whole being is so full; and the effect upon me is, in consequence, as a matter of necessity, as confusing as if it denied that I am in existence myself. If I looked into a mirror, and did not see my face, I should have the sort of feeling which actually comes upon me, when I look into this living busy world, and see no reflexion of its Creator. This is, to me, one of those great difficulties of this absolute primary truth, to which I referred just now. Were it not for this voice, speaking so clearly in my conscience and my heart, I should be an atheist, or a pantheist, or a polytheist when I looked into the world. I am speaking for myself only; and I am far from denying the real force of the arguments in proof of a God, drawn from the general facts of human society and the course of history, but these do not warm me or enlighten me; they do not take away the winter of my desolation, or make the buds unfold and the leaves grow within me, and my moral being rejoice. The sight of the world is nothing else than the prophet's scroll, full of "lamentations, and mourning, and woe."

To consider the world in its length and breadth, its various history, the many races of man, their starts, their fortunes, their mutual alienation, their conflicts; and then their ways, habits, governments, forms of worship; their enterprises, their aimless courses, their random achievements and acquirements, the impotent conclusion of long-standing facts, the tokens so faint and broken of a superintending design, the blind evolution of what turn out to be great powers or truths, the progress of things, as if from unreasoning elements, not towards final causes, the greatness and littleness of man, his far-reaching aims, his short duration, the curtain hung over his futurity, the disappointments of life, the defeat of good, the success of evil, physical pain, mental anguish, the prevalence and intensity of sin, the pervading idolatries, the corruptions, the dreary hopeless irreligion, that condition of the whole race, so fearfully yet exactly described in the Apostle's words, " having no hope and without God in the world,"—all this is a vision to dizzy and appal ; and inflicts upon the mind the sense of a profound mystery, which is absolutely beyond human solution.

What shall be said to this heart-piercing, reason-bewildering fact ? I can only answer, that either there is no Creator, or this living society of men is in a true sense discarded from His presence. Did I see a boy of good make and mind, with the tokens on him of a refined nature, cast upon the world without provision, unable to say whence he came, his birth-place, or his family connexions, I should conclude that there was some mystery connected with his history, and that he was one, of whom, from one cause or other, his parents were ashamed. Thus only should I be able to account for the contrast between the promise and the condition of his being. And so I argue about the world ;—*if* there be a God, *since* there is a God, the human race is implicated in some terrible aboriginal calamity. It is out of joint with the purposes of its Creator. This is a fact, a fact as true as the fact of its existence ; and thus the doctrine of what is theologically called original sin becomes to me almost as certain as that the world exists, and as the existence of God.

And now, supposing it were the blessed and loving will of the Creator to interfere in this anarchical condition of things, what are we to suppose would be the methods which might be necessarily or naturally involved in His purpose of mercy ? Since the world is in so abnormal a state, surely it would be no surprise to me, if the interposition were of necessity equally extraordinary—or what is called miraculous. But that subject does not directly come into the scope of my present remarks. Miracles as evidence, involve a process of reason, or an argument ; and of course I am thinking of some mode of interference which does not immediately run into argument. I

am rather asking what must be the face-to-face antagonist, by
which to withstand and baffle the fierce energy of passion and
the all-corroding, all-dissolving scepticism of the intellect in
religious inquiries ? I have no intention at all of denying, that
truth is the real object of our reason, and that, if it does not
attain to truth, either the premiss or the process is in fault ;
but I am not speaking here of right reason, but of reason as it
acts in fact and concretely in fallen man. I know that even the
unaided reason, when correctly exercised, leads to a belief in
God, in the immortality of the soul, and in a future retribution ;
but I am considering the faculty of reason actually and historically ; and in this point of view, I do not think I am wrong
in saying that its tendency is towards a simple unbelief in
matters of religion. No truth, however sacred, can stand against
it, in the long run ; and hence it is that in the pagan world,
when our Lord came, the last traces of the religious knowledge
of former times were all but disappearing from those portions
of the world in which the intellect had been active and had
had a career.

And in these latter days, in like manner, outside the Catholic
Church things are tending,—with far greater rapidity than in
that old time from the circumstance of the age,—to atheism
in one shape or other. What a scene, what a prospect, does
the whole of Europe present at this day ! and not only Europe,
but every government and every civilization through the
world, which is under the influence of the European mind !
Especially, for it most concerns us, how sorrowful, in the view
of religion, even taken in its most elementary, most attentuated
form, is the spectacle presented to us by the educated intellect
of England, France, and Germany ! Lovers of their country
and of their race, religious men, external to the Catholic Church,
have attempted various expedients to arrest fierce wilful human
nature in its onward course, and to bring it into subjection.
The necessity of some form of religion for the interests of
humanity, has been generally acknowledged : but where was
the concrete representative of things invisible, which would
have the force and the toughness necessary to be a breakwater
against the deluge ? Three centuries ago the establishment of
religion, material, legal, and social, was generally adopted as

the best expedient for the purpose, in those countries which separated from the Catholic Church ; and for a long time it was successful ; but now the crevices of those establishments are admitting the enemy. Thirty years ago, education was relied upon ; ten years ago there was a hope that wars would cease for ever, under the influence of commercial enterprise and the reign of the useful and fine arts ; but will any one venture to say that there is any thing any where on this earth, which will afford a fulcrum for us, whereby to keep the earth from moving onwards ?

The judgment, which experience passes whether on establishments or on education, as a means of maintaining religious truth in this anarchical world, must be extended even to Scripture, though Scripture be divine. Experience proves surely that the Bible does not answer a purpose for which it was never intended. It may be accidentally the means of the conversion of individuals ; but a book, after all, cannot make a stand against the wild living intellect of man, and in this day it begins to testify, as regards its own structure and contents, to the power of that universal solvent, which is so successfully acting upon religious establishments.

Supposing then it to be the Will of the Creator to interfere in human affairs, and to make provisions for retaining in the world a knowledge of Himself, so definite and distinct as to be proof against the energy of human scepticism, in such a case,—I am far from saying that there was no other way,—but there is nothing to surprise the mind, if He should think fit to introduce a power into the world, invested with the prerogative of infallibility in religious matters. Such a provision would be a direct, immediate, active, and prompt means of withstanding the difficulty ; it would be an instrument suited to the need ; and, when I find that this is the very claim of the Catholic Church, not only do I feel no difficulty in admitting the idea, but there is a fitness in it, which recommends it to my mind. And thus I am brought to speak of the Church's infallibility, as a provision, adapted by the mercy of the Creator, to preserve religion in the world, and to restrain that freedom of thought, which of course in itself is one of the greatest of our natural gifts, and to rescue it from its own suicidal excesses.

And let it be observed that, neither here nor in what follows, shall I have occasion to speak directly of Revelation in its subject-matter, but in reference to the sanction which it gives to truths which may be known independently of it,—as it bears upon the defence of natural religion. I say, that a power, possessed of infallibility in religious teaching, is happily adapted to be a working instrument, in the course of human affairs, for smiting hard and throwing back the immense energy of the aggressive, capricious, untrustworthy intellect. . . .

Apologia

THE TRIPLE OFFICE OF THE CHURCH

When our Lord went up on high, He left His representative behind Him. This was Holy Church, His mystical Body and Bride, a Divine Institution, and the shrine and organ of the Paraclete, who speaks through her till the end comes. She, to use an Anglican poet's words, is "His very self below," as far as men on earth are equal to the discharge and fulfilment of high offices, which primarily and supremely are His.

These offices, which specially belong to Him as Mediator, are commonly considered to be three ; He is Prophet, Priest, and King ; and after His pattern, and in human measure, Holy Church has a triple office too ; not the Prophetical alone and in isolation, . . . but three offices, which are indivisible, though diverse, viz. teaching, rule, and sacred ministry. . . .

Christianity, then, is at once a philosophy, a political power, and a religious rite : as a religion, it is Holy ; as a philosophy, it is Apostolic ; as a political power, it is imperial, that is, One and Catholic. As a religion, its special centre of action is pastor and flock ; as a philosophy, the Schools ; as a rule, the Papacy and its Curia.

Though it has exercised these three functions in substance from the first, they were developed in their full proportions one after another, in a succession of centuries ; first, in the primitive time it was recognized as a worship, springing up and spreading in the lower ranks of society, and among the ignorant and dependent, and making its power felt by the heroism of its Martyrs and confessors. Then it seized upon the intellectual and cultivated class, and created a theology and schools of learning. Lastly it seated itself, as an ecclesiastical polity, among princes, and chose Rome for its centre.

Truth is the guiding principle of theology and theological inquiries ; devotion and edification, of worship ; and of government, expedience. The instrument of theology is reasoning ; of worship, our emotional nature ; of rule, command and coercion. Further, in man as he is, reasoning tends to rationalism ; devotion to superstition and enthusiasm ; and power to ambition and tyranny.

Arduous as are the duties involved in these three offices, to discharge one by one, much more arduous are they to administer, when taken in combination. Each of the three has its separate scope and direction ; each has its own interests to promote and further ; each has to find room for the claims of the other two ; and each will find its own line of action influenced and modified by the others, nay, sometimes in a particular case the necessity of the others converted into a rule of duty for itself.

" Who," in St. Paul's words, " is sufficient for these things ? " Who, even with divine aid, shall successfully administer offices so independent of each other, so divergent, and so conflicting ? What line of conduct, except on the long, the very long run, is at once edifying, expedient, and true ? Is it not plain, that, if one determinate course is to be taken by the Church, acting at once in all three capacities, so opposed to each other in their idea, that course must, as I have said, be deflected from the line which would be traced out by any one of them, if viewed by itself, or else the requirements of one or two sacrificed to the interests of the third ? What, for instance, is to be done in a case when to enforce a theological point, as the Schools determine it, would make a particular population less religious, not more so, or cause riots or risings ? Or when to encourage a champion of ecclesiastical liberty in one country would encourage an Anti-Pope, or hazard a general persecution, in another ? or when either a schism is to be encountered or an opportune truth left undefined ?

All this was foreseen certainly by the Divine Mind, when He committed to His Church so complex a mission ; and, by promising her infallibility in her formal teaching, He indirectly protected her from serious error in worship and political action also. This aid, however, great as it is, does not secure her from all dangers as regards the problem which she has to solve ; nothing but the gift of impeccability granted to her authorities would secure them from all liability to mistake in their conduct, policy, words and decisions, in her legislative and her executive, in ecclesiastical and disciplinarian details ; and such a gift they have not received. In consequence, however well she may perform her duties on the whole, it will always be easy for her enemies to make a case against her, well founded or not, from the action or interaction, or the chronic collisions or contrasts, or the temporary suspense or delay, of her administration, in her three several departments of duty,—her government, her devotions, and her schools,—from the conduct of her rulers, her divines, her pastors, or her people.

*   *   *

I say, then, Theology is the fundamental and regulating principle of the whole Church system. It is commensurate with Revelation, and Revelation is the initial and essential idea of Christianity. It is the subject-matter, the formal cause, the expression, of the Prophetical Office, and, as being such, has created both the Regal Office and the Sacerdotal. And it has in a certain sense a power of jurisdiction over those offices, as being its own creations, theologians being ever in request and in employment in keeping within bounds both the political and popular elements in the Church's constitution,—elements which are far more congenial than itself to the human mind, are far more liable to excess and corruption, and are ever struggling to liberate themselves from those restraints which are in truth necessary for their well-being. . . .

Yet theology cannot always have its own way; it is too hard, too intellectual, too exact, to be always equitable, or to be always compassionate; and it sometimes has a conflict or overthrow, or has to consent to a truce or a compromise, in consequence of the rival force of religious sentiment or ecclesiastical interests; and that, sometimes in great matters, sometimes in unimportant.

*   *   *

Truth is the principle on which all intellectual, and therefore all theological inquiries proceed, and is the motive power which gives them effect; but the principle of popular edification, quickened by a keen sensitiveness of the chance of scandals, is as powerful as Truth, when the province is Religion. To the devotional mind what is new and strange is as repulsive, often as dangerous, as falsehood is to the scientific. Novelty is often error to those who are unprepared for it, from the refraction with which it enters into their conceptions. Hence popular ideas on religion are practically a match for the clearest *dicta*, deductions, and provisos of the Schools, and will have their way in cases when the particular truth, which is the subject of them, is not of vital or primary importance. Thus, in a religion, which embraces large and separate classes of adherents, there always is of necessity to a certain extent an exoteric and an esoteric doctrine. . . .

Here we see the necessary contrast between religious inquiry or teaching, and investigation in purely secular matters. Much is said in this day by men of science about the duty of honesty in what is called the pursuit of truth,—by " pursuing truth " being meant the pursuit of facts. It is just now reckoned a great moral virtue to be fearless and thorough in inquiry into facts ; and, when science crosses and breaks the received path of Revelation, it is reckoned a serious imputation upon the ethical character of religious men, whenever they show hesitation to shift at a minute's warning their position, and to accept as truths shadowy views at variance with what they have ever been taught and have held. But the contrast between the cases is plain. The love and pursuit of truth in the subject-matter of religion, if it be genuine, must always be accompanied by the fear of error, of error which may be sin. An inquirer in the province of religion is under a responsibility for his reasons and for their issue. But, whatever be the real merits, nay, virtues, of inquirers into physical or historical facts, whatever their skill, their acquired caution, their experience, their dispassionateness and fairness of mind, they do not avail themselves of these excellent instruments of inquiry as a matter of conscience, but because it is expedient, or honest, or beseeming, or praiseworthy, to use them ; nor, if in the event they were found to be wrong as to their supposed discoveries, would they, or need they, feel aught of the remorse and self-reproach of a Catholic, on whom it breaks that he has been violently handling the text of Scripture. misinterpreting it, or superseding it, on an hypothesis which he took to be true, but which turns out to be untenable.

Let us suppose in his defence that he was challenged either to admit or to refute what was asserted, and to do so without delay ; still it would have been far better could he have waited awhile, as the event has shown,—nay, far better, even though the assertion has proved true. Galileo might be right in his conclusion that the earth moves ; to consider him a heretic might have been wrong ; but there was nothing wrong in censuring abrupt, startling, unsettling, unverified disclosures, if such they were, disclosures at once uncalled for and inopportune, at a time when the limits of revealed truth had not as yet been ascertained. A man ought to be very sure of what he is saying, before he risks the chance of contradicting the word of God. It was safe, not dishonest, to be slow in accepting what nevertheless turned out to be true. Here is an instance in which the Church obliges Scripture expositors, at a given time or place, to be tender of the popular religious sense.

I have been led on to take a second view of this matter. That jealousy of originality in the matter of religion, which is the instinct of piety, is, in the case of questions which excite the popular mind, the dictate of charity also. Galileo's truth is said to have shocked and scared the Italy of his day. It revolutionized the received system of belief as regards heaven, purgatory, and hell, to say that the earth went round the sun, and it forcibly imposed upon categorical statements of Scripture, a figurative interpretation. Heaven was no longer above, and earth below ; the heavens no longer literally opened and shut ; purgatory and hell were not for certain under the earth. The catalogue of theological truths was seriously curtailed. Whither did our Lord go on His ascension ? If there is to be a plurality of worlds, what is the special importance of this one ? and is the whole visible universe with its infinite spaces, one day to pass away ? We are used to these questions now, and reconciled to them ; and on that account are no fit judges of the disorder and dismay, which the Galilean hypothesis would cause to good Catholics, as far as they became cognizant of it, or how necessary it was in charity, especially then, to delay the formal reception of a new interpretation of Scripture, till their imaginations should gradually get accustomed to it.

As to the particular measures taken at the time with this end, I neither know them accurately, nor have I any anxiety to know them. They do not fall within the scope of my argument; I am only concerned with the principle on which they were conducted. All I say is, that not all knowledge is suited to all minds; a proposition may be ever so true, yet at a particular time and place may be "temerarious, offensive to pious ears, and scandalous," though not "heretical" nor "erroneous." It must be recollected what very strong warnings we have from our Lord and St. Paul against scandalizing the weak and unintellectual. . . .

Now, while saying this, I know well . . . that, in some states of society, such as our own, it is the worst charity, and the most provoking, irritating rule of action, and the most unhappy policy, not to speak out, not to suffer to be spoken out, all that there is to say. Such speaking out is under such circumstances the triumph of religion, whereas concealment, accommodation, and evasion is to co-operate with the spirit of error;—but it is not always so. There are times and places, on the contrary, when it is the duty of a teacher, when asked, to answer frankly as well as truly, though not even then to say more than he need, because learners will but misunderstand him if he attempts more, and therefore it is wiser and kinder to let well alone, than to attempt what is better. I do not say that this is a pleasant rule of conduct, and that it would not be a relief to most men to be rid of its necessity,—and for this reason, if for no other, because it is so difficult to apply it aright, so that St. Paul's precept may be interpreted in a particular case as the warrant for just contrary courses of action,—but still, it can hardly be denied that there is a great principle in what he says, and a great duty in consequence.

Via Media I

THE ANTAGONISM BETWEEN THE CATHOLIC CHURCH AND THE WORLD

Dec. 3, 1875

I agree with you, then, but I go far beyond you in holding, that the difference between Catholics and Protestants is an ethical one ; for I think that in pure Catholics and pure Protestants (I mean, by so speaking, that most Protestants are tinged with Catholicity, and most Catholics with Protestantism) this difference is radical and immutable, as the natures of an eagle and a horse are, except logically, two things, not one. Opposition to physical science or to social and political progress, on the part of Catholics, is only an accidental and clumsy form in which this vital antagonism energises—a form, to which in its popular dress and shape, my own reason does not respond. I mean, I as little accept the associations and inferences, in which modern science and politics present themselves to the mass of Catholics, as I do those contrary ones, with which the new philosophy is coloured (I should rather say, stained) by great Professors at Belfast and elsewhere.

Dealing with facts, not with imaginations, prejudices, prepossessions, and party watchwords, I consider it historically undeniable—

1. First, that in the time of the early Roman Empire, when Christianity arose, it arose with a certain definite ethical system, which it proclaimed to be all-important, all-necessary for the present and future welfare of the human race, and of every individual member of it, and which is simply ascertainable now and unmistakable.

Next, I have a clear perception, clearer and clearer as my own experience of existing religions increases, and such as every one will share with me, who carefully examines the matter, that this ethical system ($\mathring{\eta}\theta o\varsigma$ we used to call it at Oxford as realised in individuals) is the living principle also of present Catholicism, and not of any form of Protestantism whatever—living, both as to its essential life, and also as being its vigorous motive power ; both because without it Catholicism would soon go out, and because through it Catholicism makes itself manifest, and is recognised. Outward circumstances or conditions of its presence may change or not ; the Pope may be a subject one day, a sovereign another ; *primus inter pares* in early times, the *episcopus episcoporum* now ; there might be no devotions to the Blessed Virgin formerly, they may be superabundant of late ; the Holy Eucharist might be a bare commemoration in the first century, and is a sacrifice in the nineteenth (of course I have my own definite and precise convictions of these points, but they are nothing to the purpose here, when I want to confine myself to patent facts which no one ought to dispute) ; but I say, even supposing there have been changes in doctrine and polity, still the *ethos* of the Catholic Church is what it was of old time, and whatever and whoever quarrels with Catholicism now, quarrels virtually, and would have quarrelled, if alive, 1800 years ago, with the Christianity of Apostles and Evangelists.

2. When we go on to inquire what is the ethical character, whether in Catholicity now or in Christianity in its first age, the first point to observe is that it is on all hands acknowledged to be of a character in utter variance with the ethical character of human society at large as we find it at all times. This fact is recognised, I say, by both sides, by the world and by the Church. As to the former of the two, its recognition of this antagonism is distinct and universal. As regards *Catholicism*, it is the great fact of this very day, as seen in England, France, Germany, Italy, and Spain. On the other hand, we know that in the *Apostolic* Age Christians were called the " *hostes humani generis* " (as the *Quarterly* called *Catholics* within this two years), and warred against them accordingly.

This antagonism is quite as decidedly acknowledged on the side of the Church, which calls society in reprobation " the world," and places " the world " in the number of its three enemies, with the flesh and the devil, and this in her elementary catechisms. In the first centuries her badge and boast was martyrdom ; in the fourth, as soon as she was established, her war-cry was, " *Athanasius contra mundum* " ; at a later time her protests took the shape of the Papal theocracy and the *dictatus Hildebrandi*. In the recent centuries her opposition to the world is symbolised in the history of the Jesuits. Speaking, then, according to that aspect of history which is presented to the eyes of Europeans, I say the Catholic Church is emphatically and singularly, in her relation to human philosophy and statesmanship, as was the Apostolic Church, " the Church militant here on earth."

3. And, what is a remarkable feature in her *ethos* now and at all times, she wars against the world from love of it. What, indeed, is more characteristic of what is called Romanism now than its combined purpose of opposing yet of proselytising the world ?—a combination expressed in our liturgical books by the two senses of the word " *conterere*," that of grinding down and of bringing to contrition. How strikingly, on the other hand, does this double purpose come out in the Apostles' writings ! We have three primitive documents, each quite distinct in character from the other two, differing in accidents and externals, but all intimately agreeing in substantial teaching, so that we are quite sure of the genius and spirit of Christian ethics from the first : I mean, (1) the Synoptical Gospels, (2) St. Paul's Epistles, (3) St. John's Gospel, Epistles, and Apocalypse. Now, the first of these says, " Ye shall be hated of all men for my name's sake. The disciple is not above his Master. Fear them not. I came not to send peace on earth, but a sword." " I pray not for the world," says the third, " the world hath hated them because they are not of the world. Love not the world, neither the things that are in the world. The world lieth in wickedness." And the second, " In time past ye walked according to the course of this world, and were by nature the children of wrath even as the rest." And yet, " preach the gospel to every creature," says the first ; " God so loved the world, that, etc.," says the third ; and " He will have all men to be saved," says the second. After avowals such as these in our primary authorities, it will be a hard job to discover any Irenicon between Catholicity and the moral teaching of this day.

4. This will be still clearer as we examine the details of our ethics, as developed from our fundamental principles. The

direct and prime aim of the Church is the worship of the Unseen God ; the sole object, as I may say, of the social and political world everywhere, is to make the most of this life. I do not think this antithesis an exaggeration when we look at the action of both on a large scale and in their grand outlines. In this age especially, not only are Catholics confessedly behindhand in political, social, physical, and economical science (more than they need be), but it is the great reproach urged against them by men of the world that so it is. And such a state of things is but the outcome of apostolic teaching. It was said in the beginning, " Take no thought for the morrow; Woe unto those that are rich. Blessed be the poor ; to the poor the gospel is preached. Thou hast hid these things from the wise and prudent. Not many wise men, not many mighty, not many noble are called. Many are called, few are chosen. Take up your cross and follow me. No man can have two masters ; he who loveth father or mother more than me is not worthy of me. We walk by faith, not by sight ; by faith ye are saved. This is the victory that overcometh the world, our faith. Without holiness no man can see the Lord. Our God is a consuming fire." This is a very different ethical system from that whether of Bentham or of Paley.

5. I am far from saying that it was not from the first intended that the strict and stern ethics of Christianity should be, as it was in fact, elastic enough to receive into itself secular objects and thereby secular men, and secular works and institutions, as secondary and subordinate to the *magisterium* of religion— and I am far indeed from thinking that the teaching and action of the world are unmixed evil in their first elements (society, government, law, and intellectual truth being all from God), and far from ignoring the actual goodness and excellence of individual Protestants, which comes from the same God as the Church's holiness ; but I mean that, as you might contemplate the long history of England or France, and recognise a vast difference between the two peoples in ethical character and national life, and consequent fortunes, so, and much more, you can no more make the Catholic and Protestant *ethos* one, than you can mix oil and vinegar. Catholics have a moral life

of their own, as the early Christians had, and the same life as they—our doctrines and practices come of it ; we are and always shall be militant against the world and its spirit, whether the world be considered within the Church's pale or external to it.

Contemporary Review (September, 1899)

RETROSPECT AND PROSPECT

Vi ringrazio, Monsignore, per la participazione che m' avete fatto, dell' alto onore che il Santo Padre si è degnato conferire sulla mia umile persona,—

and, if I ask your permission to continue my address to you, not in your musical language, but in my own dear mother tongue, it is because in the latter I can better express my feelings on this most gracious announcement which you have brought to me, than if I attempted what is above me.

First of all then, I am led to speak of the wonder and profound gratitude which came upon me, and which is upon me still, at the condescension and love towards me of the Holy Father in singling me out for so immense an honour. It was a great surprise. Such an elevation had never come into my thoughts, and seemed to be out of keeping with all my antecedents. I had passed through many trials, but they were over ; and now the end of all things had almost come to me, and I was at peace. And was it possible that after all I had lived through so many years for this ?

Nor is it easy to see how I *could* have borne so great a shock, had not the Holy Father resolved on a second act of condescension towards me, which tempered it, and was to all who heard of it a touching evidence of his kindly and generous nature. He felt for me, and he told me the reasons why he raised me to this high position. Besides other words of encouragement, he said his act was a recognition of my zeal and good service for so many years in the Catholic cause ; moreover, he judged it would give pleasure to English Catholics, and even to Protestant England, if I received some mark of his favour. After such gracious words from his Holiness, I should have been insensible and heartless, if I had had scruples any longer.

This is what he had the kindness to say to me, and what could I want more ? In a long course of years I have made many mistakes. I have nothing of that high perfection, which belongs to the writings of Saints, viz., that error cannot be found in them ; but what I trust that I may claim all through what I have written, is this,—an honest intention, an absence of private ends, a temper of obedience, a willingness to be corrected, a dread of error, a desire to serve Holy Church, and, through Divine Mercy, a fair measure of success. And I rejoice to say, to one great mischief I have from the first opposed myself. For 30, 40, 50 years I have resisted to the best of my powers the spirit of liberalism in religion. Never did Holy Church need champions against it more sorely than now, when, alas ! it is an error overspreading, as a snare, the whole earth; and on this great occasion, when it is natural for one who is in my place to look out upon the world, and upon Holy Church as in it, and upon her future, it will not, I hope, be considered out of place, if I renew the protest against it which I have made so often.

Liberalism in religion is the doctrine that there is no positive truth in religion, but that one creed is as good as another, and this is the teaching which is gaining substance and force daily. It is inconsistent with any recognition of any religion, as *true*. It teaches that all are to be tolerated, for all are matters of opinion. Revealed religion is not a truth, but a sentiment and a taste ; not an objective fact, not miraculous ; and it is the right of each individual to make it say just what strikes his fancy. Devotion is not necessarily founded on faith. Men may go to Protestant Churches and to Catholic, may get good from both and belong to neither. They may fraternise together in spiritual thoughts and feelings, without having any views at all of doctrine in common, or seeing the need of them. Since, then, religion is so personal a peculiarity and so private a possession, we must of necessity ignore it in the intercourse of man with man. If a man puts on a new religion every morning, what is that to you ? It is as impertinent to think about a man's religion as about his sources of income or his management of his family. Religion is in no sense the bond of society.

Hitherto the civil Power has been Christian. Even in countries separated from the Church, as in my own, the *dictum* was in force, when I was young, that : " Christianity was the law of the land." Now, every where that goodly framework of society which is the creation of Christianity is throwing off Christianity. The *dictum* to which I have referred, with a hundred others which followed upon it, is gone, or is going everywhere ; and, by the end of the century, unless the Almighty interferes, it will be *forgotten*. Hitherto, it has been considered that Religion alone, with its supernatural sanctions, was strong enough to secure submission of the masses of our population to law and order ; now the Philosophers and Politicians are bent on satisfying this problem without the aid of Christianity. Instead of the Church's authority and teaching, they would substitute first of all a universal and a thoroughly secular education, calculated to bring home to every individual that to be orderly, industrious, and sober is his personal interest. Then, for great working principles to take the place of religion, for the use of the masses thus carefully educated, it provides the broad fundamental ethical truths, of justice, benevolence, veracity, and the like ; proved experience ; and those natural laws which exist and act spontaneously in society and in social matters, whether physical or psychological ; for instance, in government, trade, finance, sanitary experiments, and the intercourse of nations. As to Religion, it is a private luxury, which a man may have if he will ; but which of course he must pay for, and which he must not obtrude upon others, or indulge in to their annoyance.

The general character of this great *apostasia* is one and the same everywhere ; but in detail, and in character, it varies in different countries. For myself, I would rather speak of it in my own country, which I know. There, I think, it threatens to have a formidable success ; though it is not easy to see what will be its ultimate issue. At first sight it might be thought that Englishmen are too religious for a movement which, on the Continent, seems to be founded on infidelity ; but the misfortune with us is, that, though it ends in infidelity as in other places, it does not necessarily arise out of infidelity. It must be recollected that the religious sects, which sprang up in England three centuries ago, and which are so powerful now, have ever been fiercely opposed to the Union of Church and State, and would advocate the unchristianizing of the monarchy and all that belongs to it, under the notion that such a catastrophe would make Christianity much more pure, and much more powerful. Next the liberal principle is forced on us from the necessity of the case. Consider what follows from the very fact of these many sects. They constitute the religion, it is supposed, of half the population ; and, recollect, our mode of government is popular. Every dozen men taken at random, whom you meet in the streets, has a share in political power,— when you inquire into their forms of belief, perhaps they represent one or other of as many as seven religions ; how can they possibly act together in municipal or in national matters, if each insists on the recognition of his own religious denomination ? All action would be at a deadlock, unless the subject of religion was ignored. We cannot help ourselves. And, thirdly, it must be borne in mind, that there is much in the liberalistic theory which is good and true ; for example, not to say more, the precepts of justice, truthfulness, sobriety, self-command, benevolence, which, as I have already noted, are among its avowed principles, and the natural laws of society. It is not till we find that this array of principles is intended to supersede, to block out, religion, that we pronounce it to be evil. There never was a device of the enemy, so cleverly framed, and with such promise of success. And already it has answered to the expectations which have been formed of it. It is sweeping into its own ranks great numbers of able, earnest, virtuous men, elderly men of approved antecedents, young men with a career before them.

Such is the state of things in England, and it is well that it should be realised by all of us ; but it must not be supposed for a moment, that I am afraid of it. I lament it deeply, because I foresee that it may be the ruin of many souls ; but I have no fear at all that it really can do aught of serious harm to the Word of God, to Holy Church, to our Almighty King, the Lion of the tribe of Judah, Faithful and True, or to His Vicar on earth. Christianity has been too often in what seemed deadly peril that we should fear for it any new trial now. So far is certain ; on the other hand, what is uncertain, and in these great contests commonly *is* uncertain, and what is commonly a great surprise, when it is witnessed, is the particular mode by which, in the event, Providence rescues and saves His elect inheritance. Sometimes our enemy is turned into a friend ; sometimes he is despoiled of that special virulence of evil which was so threatening ; sometimes he falls to pieces of himself ; sometimes he does just so much as is beneficial, and then is removed. Commonly the Church has nothing more to do than to go on in her own proper duties, in confidence and peace ; to stand still and to see the salvation of God.

Mansueti hereditabunt terram,
Et delectabuntur in multitudine pacis.

Addresses to Cardinal Newman with his Replies

THE AGE TO COME

When I would search the truths that in me burn,
  And mould them into rule and argument,
A hundred reasoners cried,—" Hast thou to learn
  Those dreams are scatter'd now, those fires are spent ? "
And, did I mount to simpler thoughts, and try
Some theme of peace, 'twas still the same reply.

Perplex'd, I hoped my heart was pure of guile,
  But judged me weak in wit, to disagree ;
But now, I see that men are mad awhile,
  And joy the age to come will think with me :—
'Tis the old history—Truth without a home,
Despised and slain, then rising from the tomb.

                              Verses on Various Occasions

A FINAL MESSAGE TO A NON-CATHOLIC

January 29, 1890.

MY DEAR MR. EDWARDS,—Accept my tardy Christmas greetings and good wishes to you for fulness in faith, hope, charity, gladness and peace ; for the blessings of Holy Church, and of Gospel gifts, for the Communion of Saints, and the Life Everlasting.

I shall venture to send you what I may call my Creed over-leaf.

Yours most truly,

J. H. N.

MY CREED

Soul of Christ, be my sanctification ;
Body of Christ, be my salvation ;
Blood of Christ, fill all my veins ;
Water of Christ's side, wash out my stains ;
Passion of Christ, my comfort be ;
O good Jesu, listen to me ;
In Thy wounds I fain would hide,
Ne'er to be parted from Thy side ;
Guard me, should the foe assail me ;
Call me when my life shall fail me ;
Bid me come to Thee above,
With Thy Saints to sing Thy love,
World without end. AMEN.

Meditations and Devotions

THE DIVINE PROVIDENCE AND
THE INDIVIDUAL

1. God was all-complete, all-blessed in Himself; but it was His will to create a world for His glory. He is Almighty, and might have done all things Himself, but it has been His will to bring about His purposes by the beings He has created. We are all created to His glory—we are created to do His will. I am created to do something or to be something for which no one else is created; I have a place in God's counsels, in God's world, which no one else has; whether I be rich or poor, despised or esteemed by man, God knows me and calls me by my name.

2. God has created me to do Him some definite service; He has committed some work to me which He has not committed to another. I have my mission—I never may know it in this life, but I shall be told it in the next. Somehow I am necessary for His purposes, as necessary in my place as an Archangel in His—if, indeed, I fail, He can raise another, as He could make the stones children of Abraham. Yet I have a part in this great work; I am a link in a chain, a bond of connexion between persons. He has not created me for naught. I shall do good, I shall do His work; I shall be an angel of peace, a preacher of truth in my own place, while not intending it, if I do but keep His commandments and serve Him in my calling.

3. Therefore I will trust Him. Whatever, wherever I am, I can never be thrown away. If I am in sickness, my sickness may serve Him; in perplexity, my perplexity may serve Him; if I am in sorrow, my sorrow may serve Him. My sickness, or perplexity, or sorrow may be necessary causes of some great end, which is quite beyond us. He does nothing in vain; He may prolong my life, He may shorten it; He knows what He is about. He may take away my friends, He may throw me among strangers, He may make me feel desolate, make my spirits sink, hide the future from me—still He knows what He is about.

O Adonai, O Ruler of Israel, Thou that guidest Joseph like a flock, O Emmanuel, O Sapientia, I give myself to Thee. I trust Thee wholly. Thou art wiser than I—more loving to me than I myself. Deign to fulfil Thy high purposes in me whatever they be—work in and through me. I am born to serve Thee, to be Thine, to be Thy instrument. Let me be Thy blind instrument. I ask not to see—I ask not to know—I ask simply to be used.

Meditations and Devotions

PROFESSION OF FAITH

A

Such is the infallibility lodged in the Catholic Church, viewed in the concrete, as clothed and surrounded by the appendages of its high sovereignty : it is, to repeat what I said above, a supereminent prodigious power sent upon earth to encounter and master a giant evil.

And now, having thus described it, I profess my own absolute submission to its claim. I believe the whole revealed dogma as taught by the Apostles, as committed by the Apostles to the Church, and as declared by the Church to me. I receive it, as it is infallibly interpreted by the authority to whom it is thus committed, and (implicitly) as it shall be, in like manner, further interpreted by that same authority till the end of time. I submit, moreover, to the universally received traditions of the Church, in which lies the matter of those new dogmatic definitions which are from time to time made, and which in all times are the clothing and the illustration of the Catholic dogma as already defined. And I submit myself to those other decisions of the Holy See, theological or not, through the organs which it has itself appointed, which, waiving the question of their infallibility, on the lowest ground come to me with a claim to be accepted and obeyed. Also, I consider that, gradually and in the course of ages, Catholic inquiry has taken certain definite shapes, and has thrown itself into the form of a science, with a method and a phraseology of its own, under the intellectual handling of great minds, such as St. Athanasius, St. Augustine, and St. Thomas ; and I feel no temptation at all to break in pieces the great legacy of thought thus committed to us for these latter days.

Apologia

B

I die in the faith of the One Holy Catholic Apostolic Church. I trust I shall die prepared and protected by her Sacraments, which our Lord Jesus Christ has committed to her, and in that communion of Saints which He inaugurated when He ascended on high, and which will have no end. I hope to die in that Church which our Lord founded on Peter, and which will continue till His second coming.

I commit my soul and body to the Most Holy Trinity, and to the merits and grace of our Lord Jesus, God Incarnate, to the intercession and compassion of our dear Mother Mary ; to St. Joseph ; and St. Philip Neri, my father, the father of an unworthy son ; to St. John the Evangelist ; St. John the Baptist ; St. Henry ; St. Athanasius, and St. Gregory Nazianzen ; to St. Chrysostom, and St. Ambrose.

Also to St. Peter, St. Gregory I., and St. Leo. Also to the great Apostle, St. Paul.

Also to my tender Guardian Angel, and to all Angels, and to all Saints.

And I pray to God to bring us all together again in heaven, under the feet of the Saints. And, after the pattern of Him, who seeks so diligently for those who are astray, I would ask Him especially to have mercy on those who are external to the True Fold, and to bring them into it before they die.

Meditations and Devotions

IN PROSPECT OF THE END

Times come and go, and man will not believe, that that is to be which is not yet, or that what now is only continues for a season, and is not eternity. The end is the trial ; the world passes ; it is but a pageant and a scene ; the lofty palace crumbles, the busy city is mute, the ships of Tarshish have sped away. On heart and flesh death is coming ; the veil is breaking. Departing soul, how hast thou used thy talents, thy opportunities, the light poured around thee, the warnings given thee, the grace inspired into thee ? O my Lord and Saviour, support me in that hour in the strong arms of Thy Sacraments, and by the fresh fragrance of Thy consolations. Let the absolving words be said over me, and the holy oil sign and seal me, and Thy own Body be my food, and Thy Blood my sprinkling ; and let my sweet Mother Mary breathe on me, and my Angel whisper peace to me, and my glorious Saints, and my own dear Father, Philip, smile on me ; that in them all, and through them all, I may receive the gift of perseverance, and die, as I desire to live, in Thy faith, in Thy Church, in Thy service, and in Thy love.

Discourses to Mixed Congregations

THE APPARENT AND THE REAL

What principally attracted me in the ante-Nicene period was the great Church of Alexandria, the historical centre of teaching in those times. Of Rome for some centuries comparatively little is known. The battle of Arianism was first fought in Alexandria ; Athanasius, the champion of the truth, was Bishop of Alexandria ; and in his writings he refers to the great religious names of an earlier date, to Origen, Dionysius, and others, who were the glory of its see, or of its school. The broad philosophy of Clement and Origen carried me away ; the philosophy, not the theological doctrine ; and I have drawn out some features of it in my volume, with the zeal and freshness, but with the partiality, of a neophyte. Some portions of their teaching, magnificent in themselves, came like music to my inward ear, as if the response to ideas, which, with little external to encourage them, I had cherished so long. These were based on the mystical or sacramental principle, and spoke of the various economies or Dispensations of the Eternal. I understood these passages to mean that the exterior world, physical and historical, was but the manifestation to our senses of realities greater than itself. Nature was a parable : Scripture was an allegory : pagan literature, philosophy, and mythology, properly understood, were but a preparation for the Gospel. The Greek poets and sages were in a certain sense prophets ; for " thoughts beyond their thought to those high bards were given." There had been a directly divine dispensation granted to the Jews ; but there had been in some sense a dispensation carried on in favour of the Gentiles. He who had taken the seed of Jacob for His elect people had not therefore cast the rest of mankind out of His sight. In the fulness of time both Judaism and Paganism had come to nought ; the outward frame-work, which concealed yet suggested the Living Truth, had never been intended to last, and it was dissolving under the beams of the Sun of Justice which shone behind it and through it. The process of change had been slow ; it had been done not rashly, but by rule and measure, " at sundry times and in divers manners," first one disclosure and then another, till the whole evangelical doctrine was brought into full manifestation. And thus room was made for the anticipation of further and deeper disclosures, of truths still under the veil of the letter, and in their season to be revealed. The visible world still remains without its divine interpretation ; Holy Church in her sacraments and her hierarchical appointments, will remain, even to the end of the world, after all but a symbol of those heavenly facts which fill eternity. Her mysteries are but the expressions in human language of truths to which the human mind is unequal. It is evident how much there was in all this in correspondence with the thoughts which had attracted me when I was young, and with the doctrine which I have already associated with the Analogy and the Christian Year.

Apologia

WRITTEN IN PROSPECT OF DEATH

If a tablet is put up in the cloister, such as the three there already, I should like the following, if good Latinity, and if there is no other objection : *e.g.* it must not be if persons to whom I should defer thought it sceptical. [J. H. N., *Feb.* 13, 1881]

JOANNES HENRICUS NEWMAN

EX UMBRIS ET IMAGINIBUS

IN VERITATEM

DIE — — A.S. 18

Requiescat in pace

My only difficulty is St. Paul, Heb. x. 1, where he assigns " umbra " to the Law—but surely, though we have in many respects an εἰκών of the Truth, there is a good deal of σκιά still, as in the doctrine of the Holy Trinity.

Meditations and Devotions

EPILOGUE

The application of this vision to Martin's age is obvious ; I suppose it means in this day, that Christ comes not in pride of intellect, or reputation for philosophy. These are the glittering robes in which Satan is now arraying. Many spirits are abroad, more are issuing from the pit ; the credentials which they display are the precious gifts of mind, beauty, richness, depth, originality. Christian, look hard at them with Martin in silence, and ask them for the print of the nails.

Historical Sketches **II**